JESUS . . . WHO?

John R. Brokhoff

JESUS ... WHO?

ISBN 0-89536-116-7
PRINTED IN U.S.A.

Dedicated with love to —
Wendy B. Shook
Helen B. Landel
Virginia B. Waits
Jodi B. Platz

CONTENTS

Foreword: O for a Tongue!

To praise the Redeemer, Charles Wesley exclaimed, "O for a thousand tongues . . ." Today's charismatic movement is calling upon the church to speak in tongues. It may be all right to have a thousand tongues to praise the Lord and it may be all right to speak in various kinds of tongues to express the Spirit. But, what the church needs today is not many tongues but *one* tongue. If the church had only one tongue, it would be enough to renew the church and win the world. The church today would be better off if she put less emphasis on tongues and became concerned about one tongue. In light of the world situation, we must exclaim, "Oh, if only the church could recover her tongue!"

Since we are about to enter the Pentecost season, we need to be reminded that Pentecost was a tongue affair. The Spirit came in the form of cloven tongues of fire. The crowd heard the disciples speaking in foreign tongues. Peter used his tongue to preach the first Christian sermon. Pentecost was a communicatin event. The Holy Spirit used the tongue of the disciples to proclaim the good news of the gospel. If the gospel is to be preached today, the Spirit is indispensible to the point of no Spirit, no witnessing.

The Spirit Behind the Tongue

An examination of the account of the Pentecost experience in Acts 2:1-21 shows that the Spirit makes it possible for one to use the tongue to preach. The account says, "They were all filled with the Holy Spirit and began to speak in other tongues, as the Spirit gave them utterance." To speak you need more than a tongue. You need wind, forced air produced by the diaphragm, to pass through the voice box to make a sound. The tongue is used to control the sound in making words. The

Hebrew word for "spirit" is *rauch*, meaning "breath." The Spirit came like a rushing, mighty wind. Jesus referred to the Spirit as the wind. Thus, word and spirit belong together inseparably. You cannot say a word without breath (spirit). Luther said, "God will not give you his Spirit apart from the external word." Paul agrees: "And take the sword of the Spirit which is the word of God." This means that to speak, to communicate, to witness, and to preach we must have the Spirit.

The Spirit is the wind that makes speaking possible. I learned this lesson some time ago when I was sailing on a Florida bay. To go from one end of the bay to another I had to go under several highway bridges. Since the the mast was too high to go under a bridge, I wondered how I could get the drawbridge to open up and let me through. One day I asked an operator of a bridge what I had to do to get through. He told me that I had to sound a horn that could be heard a mile away. I hastened to a marine supply store to buy a horn which, since it had to be heard a mile away, I thought was going to be quite a sizeable horn. The salesman sold me a horn which looked like a child's toy and with it a can of compressed air. Since I had doubts whether that little horn could be heard a mile away, I began to experiment when I got home to the garage. I attached the can of air to the horn and pressed the button. And the blast was so great that I almost broke my eardrums! The horn itself was as small as a toy, but the compressed air made it sound for a mile!

This is what happens in preaching and personal witnessing. The Spirit makes us sound forth in a mighty way, telling of the wonderful work of God on our behalf in Jesus. The fact is that no person can proclaim apart from the Spirit; he has no air to make a sound. When Jesus preached his first sermon, his text was "The Spirit of the Lord is upon me because he has anointed me to preach good news . . ." God through Joel said, "I will pour out my Spirit upon all flesh, and your sons and your daughters shall prophesy . . ." When the Spirit possesses you, there is no keeping quiet. On the first Palm Sunday the children were so filled with the spirit of praise that "if these should be silent the very stones would cry out."

Having the Spirit is the key to witnessing to the unchurched. In recent years major denominations, alarmed at their declining membership, have become interested in evangelism again. One gets the impression that evangelism is based on projects, programs, and promotion. We set up quotas of how many new members each congregation is expected to gain. We spend hundreds of thousands of dollars on literature for use in winning converts. Evangelism is not a project or program that can be put on at special times for special emphasis. Evangelism is for all time or it is for no time. When a Christian has experienced Christ and has received the Spirit, he cannot help telling the good news to all who will listen. He does not go out to witness as a duty to build up the church's membership. He witnesses normally, naturally, spontaneously, and constantly because the Spirit gives him utterance. The Spirit impels, motivates, and drives him to win others to Christ. This is not only the preacher's task. It is the privilege of every Christian. But how many church members make an effort to witness to non-Christians? In the average church the number is pitifully small. This means that the success of evangelism depends upon a fresh outpouring of the Spirit upon the members of the church including the pastor.

The Spirit that gives the laity utterance to witness is the same Spirit that gives preachers unction in their preaching. The lack of Spirit makes a sermon deadly dull. Many preachers give the impression that they could not care less about what they are saying. It seems that preachers are not in it, nor with it. The gospel does not appear to be a life-and-death matter. Many preachers lack enthusiasm in their preaching. The word, "enthusiasm" means "God in us." Unless God the Spirit is in us, we will not get excited, aroused, and zealous about our preaching the Word. Lincoln expressed the way many people feel about sermons. He said, "When I hear a man preach, I like to see him act as if he were fighting bees." A black preacher explained his method, "First I explains the text, then I presents the arguments, then I puts in the rousements." The Spirit gives the "rousements," the excitement, resulting in your saying, "Have you heard the good news? Let me tell you about it! Isn't that great news?"

The Spirit Makes Sense

We have seen that forced air going through the voice box makes a sound. But what kind of a sound? Will it make sense to those who hear it? What we say must make sense if we are going to communicate the gospel. Today some are saying that the Spirit makes one speak in unknown tongues, in languages and words which no one can understand. In the first Pentecostal experience it needs to be pointed out that the disciples did not speak in unknown tongues but in foreign tongues so that foreign visitors in Jerusalem might be able to understand the gosepl. For uneducated men to speak a foreign language is a miracle. If you have struggled with a foreign language through college and seminary, you know how difficult it is to even read a foreign language, not to mention to speak it fluently. Pentecost was not a time for the Spirit's speaking in unknown but in known and intelligible tongues. Speaking by the Spirit and in response to the Spirit does not always mean speaking in unknown tongues. It may happen very rarely. The Spirit normally is expressed by clear, sensible, and intelligible language for all to understand and accept. The purpose of the Spirit is not to hide the truth but to make the truth plain, for one function of the Spirit is to enlighten us in the truth.

One of the problems Christians have today is speaking in people's language. The problem is faced by every church school teacher who must be able to speak in a way that children will understand. The preacher also has the problem of putting the gospel in a language that will be clear to the teenager as well as the PhD who sits on the same pew. When we preach, we must not be content to speak our professional language but the language of the people assembled for worship. This means that we who share the gospel either individually or corporately must use the proper language. In our vanity we may be tempted to use big words unknown to the average person. How many in an average congregation would understand words like these: paraenesis, nubile, acerbate, irascible, pellucid, and pyrrhic?

In our communicating, we need the Holy Spirit to make the gospel crystal clear. Some may like to show off their intelligence by making the message as obscure as possible by using big words and involved sentences. At Caesarea Philippi Jesus asked the disciples who they thought he was. Peter answered, "You are the Christ, the Son of the living God." If Peter spoke like some contemporary folks, he would have answered: "You are the eschatological manifestation of the ground of our being, the kerygma in which we find the ultimate meaning of our interpersonal relationships." And Jesus would respond, "What?" A sign of the Spirit's possession is simplicity and clarity in proclaiming the gospel. It takes a truly intelligent person to make the truth simple but yet profound. An obscure speech indicates an obscure mind of the speaker. Phillips Brooks said that one of the highest compliments he ever received was from a newspaper boy who attended his church every Sunday. Mystified by the boy's presence, Brooks sent a layman to ask the boy why he came. The lad explained, "Oh, I like to hear Dr. Brooks. You see, he doesn't know any more than I do!"

What to Say

As we enter the Pentecost season, we are reminded that Pentecost is a communications event. The Spirit makes it possible for us to speak the truth of the Word. The Spirit enlightens us in the meaning of the Word so that we can speak it clearly and simply. Now we come to the point of the content of our message. How can we communicate as Christians to non-Christians if we do not have anything to say? What is the sense of calling up a friend if you have nothing to talk about? Why have a TV station if there are no programs to be presented? On the first Pentecost the disciples had something to say. In the Acts account, it says, "We hear them telling in their own tongues the mighty works of God."

One problem in our preaching and witnessing is that we do not have anything worthwhile to say. People leave church sometimes feeling they got nothing out of the sermon and that they may as well have stayed home. Sometimes we just give a diagnosis of a sick society without having a prescription. We raise questions in the pulpit and have no answers. People come for bread and they get stones. The crisis of today's pulpit is the crisis of theology.

Connected with not having anything to communicate is having the wrong things to say, our contemporary heresies. Bishop E. K. Leslie summed it up: "They appear to offer up a theology without God, a creation without a Creator, a natural world without a supernatural background, an eternal present without a hereafter, a morality without morals, a hopeless humanity without a Redeemer, a church without a Holy Spirit, a priesthood without sacrifice, a Jesus of Nazareth without his heavenly Father, Christ the servant without Christ the Savior."

What is there to say? The Holy Spirit is the answer. He guides and leads into truth. Jesus promised the Spirit would do this for us. The Spirit gave Peter the content of his message that brought three thousand people to a decision for Christ. His sermon told of what God had done in the past for his people. Then he told what God did during these days in the cross and resurrection of Jesus. Then he brought it down to the very day of receiving the Spirit and explained what happened.

Today the Spirit gives us content for our communication. It is the Bible. This book is the product of the Holy Spirit who used holy men to write the revelation of God. In the Bible the Spirit gives us wisdom to deal with our problems. In and through the Bible the Spirit gives answers to our questions and solutions for our problems. This explains why church school teachers use the Bible as the source of their teaching. This is why preachers, who are true to the Word, engage in biblical preaching. The Spirit tells us what to say and what to preach through the Scriptures.

The time has come for the church to stop worrying about speaking in tongues and to stop hoping for a thousand tongues to sing praises to God. These many tongues can lead us only into the utter confusion of a tower of Babel. What we need today is one tongue, one voice, coming from the Holy Spirit. If only the church could regain her voice! If only each Christian would be concerned about using his one tongue! God gave each of us only one tongue. Let's use it to tell the good news of Jesus. But, we can't do this alone; we must have the Holy Spirit. So we pray, "Come Holy Ghost, our souls inspire."

A Matter of Life and Breath
Pentecost I

On the evening of that day, the first day of the week, the doors being shut where the disciples were, for fear of the Jews, Jesus came and stood among them and said to them, "Peace be with you." When he had said this, he showed them his hands and his side. Then the disciples were glad when they saw the Lord. Jesus said to them again, "Peace be with you. As the Father has sent me, even so I send you." And when he had said this, he breathed on them, and said to them, "Receive the Holy Spirit. If you forgive the sins of any, they are forgiven; if you retain the sins of any, they are retained." [John 20:19-23.]

It is a matter of life and death if you do not have breath. A cigarette ad warns against smoking which causes one to breathe tar into the lungs. It is a warning against lung cancer. Whether or not you smoke can be a matter of life and breath.

Life and breath go together. The common saying is that if you are not breathing, you are dead. One must breathe to live. This is also true in the spiritual sense. The Hebrew word for spirit is *rauch*, meaning "breath." After Adam was created physically, God breathed into his nostrils the breath of life, and Adam became a "living being." When Ezekiel saw Israel as a valley of dry bones, God called upon the Spirit to "breathe upon these slain that they may live." On Easter night Jesus came to the Disciples and "breathed on them" and said, "Receive the Holy Spirit."

The breath of God gives life; the Spirit of God causes birth. This Pentecost Sunday is celebrated by the universal church as the birthday of the church. The church came to life, to existence, when the Holy Spirit came upon the Disciples. Under the impact of the Spirit, Peter preached the first Christian sermon and 3,000 joined the church. The church is the product of the Spirit. She is a divine, not human, institution. The church is of God and consists of God's people called together by the Spirit. Born of the Spirit the church had its first birthday almost 2,000 years ago. But what about this year? Does the church — your church — need a new birth? If so, then she needs a fresh experience with the Spirit. Once again Jesus needs to come to us disciples, breathe on us, and say, "Receive the Holy Spirit."

A Disheartened Church Comes Alive

Our text tells us how the church can come alive again. The first step to be taken is for the church to receive from Christ the Holy Spirit. On Easter night Jesus came to the Eleven who in fear had shut themselves behind locked doors. They were disillusioned, distraught, and discouraged. They were about as low as they could get, because they thought their cause had ended on the cross. They must have felt like Charlie Brown who comes to a psychiatric stand manned by Lucy. He has problems and he moans, "I've never felt more low in all my life." He explains that everything he tries turns to disaster. He has had an unbroken string of failures. Lucy offers him some wisdom, "People are like a deck of cards. We're all part of the deck. Some are aces, others are tens or nines or twos. We can't all be face cards, can we? We can't all be kings and queens." Charlie agrees, and Lucy goes on, "Maybe you're the two of clubs, Charlie Brown." This doesn't help, for Charlie responds, "I doubt it. Even the two of clubs takes a trick now and then."

Today's church is much like that today. On the whole church people are lifeless, disinterested, and indifferent to the cause and work of the church. One almost feels like taking a local church by the shoulders, shaking it, and saying, "Come alive, church!" Facts about the average church bear this out. Seventy-five percent of the work of the local church is done by twenty-five percent of the members. How much life is there when an average of forty percent of the members is inactive? On any given Sunday morning, only thirty to forty percent of the church people come to worship. The church lacks Spirit and, therefore, lacks life.

In today's gospel we see that Christ comes to this disheartened church. He comes to give the disciples the Holy Spirit to bring them out of the doldrums and to set them on fire with zeal for the gospel. Note that Christ gives the Spirit not, in this case, to individuals but to the group assembled in the Upper Room. When we think of receiving the Spirit, we usually think of the Spirit's coming to an individual. This is not always the case. Getting the Spirit is not always a private or an individual affair. The coming of the Spirit can be a corporate experience. Indeed, each disciple received the Spirit, but he received him as a part of the group, the church. This indicates to each of us that if we want a fresh outpouring of the Spirit, he will come to us as we assemble together for prayer and worship. If you want the Spirit, go to God's house and join your fellow-Christians in worship.

Note, too, that the Spirit came to the disciples on this occasion in a very normal and orderly fashion. Here again we need to be reminded that the Spirit does not come always as commonly believed. Many think the Spirit comes in a very dramatic and unusual way. We think of his coming as an intense emotional experience. We expect to hear bells ringing, to see angels, to hear voices, and to be touched with tongues of fire. As in the case of Saul, this may happen: a fall from his horse, blinded by intense light, and hearing the voice of Jesus. This is exceptional. For most of us the Spirit comes as he came to the original disciples. In his own words, C. S. Lewis, author of many excellent Christian books, tells of his conversion: "You must picture me alone in that room in Magdalen, night after night, feeling, whenever my

mind lifted for even a second from my work, the steady,
unrelenting approach of him whom I so earnestly desired
not to meet. That which I greatly feared had at last come
upon me." Then he knelt down in prayer and admitted
that God was God. He says he felt "the most dejected and
reluctant convert in all England."

How does Christ give the Spirit to us, his disciples?
As it was with the first disciples, the Spirit came with
Jesus' presence. Our text says, "Jesus came and stood
among them." He identified himself as the real Jesus of
Nazareth who died on the cross: "He showed them his
hands and his side." Christ comes to give the Spirit. This
helps us to know who the Spirit is. He is not a ghost to
frighten us. He is not a mystery to confound us. The Holy
Spirit is none other than the spirit of Christ. To have the
Holy Spirit is to have the spirit of Christ in our hearts.
This spirit of Christ is the spirit demonstrated in his life
on earth: love, joy, peace . . .

Christ gives the Spirit to us, also, through his words.
"He breathed on them, and said to them, 'Receive the
Holy Spirit.' " In a marvelous and mysterious way the
Spirit comes in and through the spoken word of Jesus.
This is not an isolated instance. You will remember that
the Spirit came upon the people in Jerusalem as they
listened to Peter's sermon on Pentecost. When Peter
later preached to Cornelius and his friends, Acts reports,
"While Peter was still saying this, the Holy Spirit fell on
all who heard the word." The Word and the Spirit are
one. As water fills a sponge, the Spirit comes into and is
possessed by the Word. The Spirit is identified with the
Word of God. Paul put it this way, "Take the sword of
the Spirit which is the Word of God." This should help
those of us who want a fuller measure of Spirit. He will
come to us when we devote ourselves to the Word: as we
read it devotionally, listen to it taught in a classroom, or
as we receive it from a pulpit. This is one of the major
reasons for going to church every Sunday. It is to hear
the Word which brings the Spirit to those whose hearts

are open. If the church is to have a new birth, a genuine renewal of spirit, then the church must once more preach powerfully the Word and people must pack the churches to hear that Word. Then, the church will again come alive.

The Power To Be and To do

If the church is to come alive again on this Pentecost Sunday, the church must take a second step of using the power which comes from the Spirit. In our text, just before he breathed the Spirit upon the disciples, Jesus gave the church the greatest task and challenge ever given to a group of people. He said, "As the Father has sent me, even so I send you." Jesus gave to the church the same mission as the Father gave him to accomplish on earth. Where will the power come from to do this herculean task? This Christian's power comes from the Spirit. Before ascending to the Father, Jesus told his men, "You shall receive power when the Holy Spirit has come upon you."

Before we seek to know more about the power to do the job, we had better be sure we know what Jesus is asking us, the church, to do. What is the purpose of the church? What is your local congregation living for? What do you conceive your mission to be in your community? The primary purpose of the church is not to educate people. Nor is it the primary purpose of God's people to heal people physically or psychologically. It is not the primary purpose of the church to feed people nor to make them physically comfortable. It is not even the primary purpose of the church to make men good. What then is the primary purpose? It is to reconcile people to God, to bring sinners to repentance. Jesus said it was his mission to seek the lost and give his life a ransom. The weakness of today's church is in the fact that we have been concerned primarily with personal ethics and social action to the neglect of bringing people to God. When the

Church fulfills her primary divine purpose, and men and women are thereby rightly related to God, the secondary purposes of the church will be fulfilled. It is therefore timely and appropriate that in these years the church should make as its emphasis evangelism and world missions.

But man cannot carry out this mission given by Christ to the church all by himself. He must have the power of God to bring it to pass. Christ does not give us only an impossible task but he makes available for us the means to do it. This power is in the Spirit which he breathed upon the apostles, and will breathe upon us on this Pentecost Day. What is this power? It is none less than the power of God. We all know that God is almighty, an omnipotent being. Nothing is impossible with God. The Holy Spirit has the same ability because he is the third person of the Trinity. To have the Spirit is to have the power of almighty God at our disposal. Thus, Paul could write, "I can do all things through Christ who strengthens me."

Let us be sure, though, that we understand the difference between power and force. God's power at our disposal is not the power to send a man to Mars. A son who was a chemist working on the development of rocket fuel called his father, a Seminary professor, after the successful launching of the first man-bearing satellite. He asked, "Dad, did you see it? Wasn't that real power?" The father replied, "No, that wasn't real power." "What do you mean that wasn't real power?" "That was force," replied the father, "when that rocket went up not one broken home was mended, not one drunken man was sobered, not one sinful life was changed — that takes real power." The power the Spirit gives us is the power to bring men to Christ, to turn doubt to faith, to turn sinners into saints.

If this is true, why then is the average Christian and the average local church apparently impotent and lifeless, doing little to nothing, hardly ever growing in numbers or in spirituality? It is a case of the tragic non-use of the power available in the Spirit. It is said that a man once went into a hardware store and looked at a power chain saw. The salesman told him that it could cut so many cords of wood in a day. The man bought it but came back about a week later. He wanted his money back because he said he worked all day cutting wood with the saw but could not even get one cord by the end of the day. The salesman took the saw, turned on the switch, and cranked it up. There was a roar in the salesroom. The customer was amazed. He was cutting wood without having turned on the power. This can and does happen to many Christians like you and me. This tremendous supply of power to change life is at our fingertips, but we fail to turn on the switch. And that switch is faith. Turn on the switch of faith and God's power at once begins to work in and through you to witness, to win, to overcome.

No Salvation Outside The Church?

You and your church can come alive on this Pentecost Sunday if you allow the Spirit to use you to forgive. After saying "Receive the Holy Spirit," Jesus gave them an authority usually reserved for God himself. Jesus continued, "If you forgive the sins of any, they are forgiven; if you retain the sins of any, they are retained."

Here is a difficult thing for many of us to understand. How can we human beings have the authority and power to forgive and retrain sins? Is this not what only God can do? We may be able to forgive sins committed against us, but can we forgive sins that have been committed against God? It is not man who forgives but it is the Spirit who forgives through the church. In explaining the doctrine of the Spirit, the third article of the Apostles' Creed, Luther says, "In this Christian church day after day he (Holy Spirit) fully forgives my sins and the sins of all believers." The Christian then is only the instrument the Spirit uses to forgive.

This implies then that the church was given the authority to forgive sins through the Spirit. Who constitutes the church: clergy or laity? Our answer will determine whether laymen and clergymen, or both, may pronounce forgiveness. For instance, do you as a member of the church feel you could tell someone that he is forgiven? Or, do you think that only an ordained clergyman may give absolution with genuine authority? Let us go back to the original, back to the text. To whom did Jesus say this? He said it to the disciples, the whole church at that time. There was no division at that time between laity and clergy. The church is the whole people of God, clerical and lay.

There is no question whether the ordained clergyman has the authority to be a spokesman of the Spirit when he says, "I declare unto you the entire forgiveness of all your sins." Every true minister of the gospel feels that these words are the most important he has to say in his entire ministry. He can say it truly because Christ gave the Spirit who works and speaks through him. He can say it because the church at his ordination gave him the authority to declare absolution.

How about you, the layman? Can you be used by the Spirit to forgive others? A devout Christian woman had a conversation with a disturbed friend who was upset about her life. The Christian said what she needed to do was to confess her sin and get absolution. Then she would have peace. The friend suggested that she confess her sins right then and there and get absolution. The Christian lady said she did not feel qualified because she was no minister. She advised her friend to go to her pastor and get absolution. The friend replied, "But I can't go to him, for I would be embarrassed to tell him what I did." The friend persisted in her desire to confess, so the Christian woman heard the confession and then assured her that God forgave her on the basis of her repentance and faith. Was this not in keeping with what Jesus had in mind when he said, "If you forgive the sins of any, they are forgiven?"

Another implication of what we are talking about is that salvation (forgiveness) is found in the church as the Spirit forgives through church people, both laity and clergy. The Spirit forgives in and through the church. He comes to us by Word and Sacraments — Baptism and the Lord's Supper. We have already seen that the Spirit comes with the Word, and the Word constitutes a sacrament with an earthly element as an outward sign. This brings us to the logical conclusion to which many object: "There is no salvation outside the Christian church." This was the claim of St. Cyprian as far back as the 4th century. Luther in the 16th century taught it: "Outside the Christian church there is no truth, no Christ, no salvation." And it needs to be preached and taught and lived in the 20th century, for this conviction is the foundation of our entire program of winning others to Christ both in our neighborhood and throughout the world.

When the president of Liberia, William Tolbert, had a birthday recently, he went off into the jungle and spent the night in the village of Joundi. He asked the pastors and church leaders to meet with him at 6 a.m. to begin his birthday with Bible study and prayer. He used his birthday to get re-born in the Spirit. Today is the church's birthday. Because we are the church, it is our birthday, too. Is it not appropriate for us to be like the Disciples in the Upper Room to await again the presence and words of Jesus giving us anew the Spirit? Since he comes to breathe on us the Spirit, each needs to pray:

Breathe on me, breath of God
Till I am wholly Thine,
Till every earthly part of me
Glows with Thy fire divine.

Our Three-Faced God
Trinity

"Go therefore and make disciples of all nations, baptizing them in the name of the Father and of the Son and of the Holy Spirit." [*Matthew 28:19.*]

In my home town, Pottsville, Pennsylvania, where I grew up as a boy, there is the county courthouse situated on one of the hills. Arising out of the center of the building was a high tower with a clock on it. The clock had four faces to enable townspeople to see the time from any direction. As a boy, I was always captivated by the clock because I wondered whether there were four clocks each with a face or whether there was one clock with four faces. If there was one clock with four faces, it was a mystery to me how that could work.

On this Trinity Sunday we are confronted with the mystery of the Holy Trinity. Most of us react to the Trinity in terms of being frightened by God, confused by Christ, and puzzled by the Holy Spirit. Perhaps it would help us to overcome our confusion if we would consider the Trinity in terms of the courthouse clock with four faces. We can say that our God is a three-faced God: God the Father, God the Son, and God the Holy Spirit. This God-clock does not have three separate clocks, one for each face. There is only one clock which has three faces. There is only God and Three persons as Father, Son, and Holy Spirit. The three are God. Each face tells us the "time" about God. We can enter into the nature of God through the Father, or the Son, or the Holy Spirit. This is the threefold nature of God into which we are baptized. Jesus' final direction to his church was to baptize the world in the name of the Father, Son, and Holy Spirit. If we were so baptized, then we need to know what this trinitarian formula means and implies.

The Face of God the Father

The first face we see is God the Father whom we are to fear. The church was commanded to baptize converts into the name of the Father-God. In the last decade there has been so much emphasis upon the love of God that we have lost the fear of God. We are to fear God not in terms of being afraid of him but in terms of respect, awe, reverence, and adoration.

This fear of God is based upon the greatness of God. In the last few years we have been singing not "How great thou are" but how great man is. We have been putting God into man's limitations. We have made God one of us as a friend and brother. We have been told that we should find God in human beings. God has become very human, very much like us rather than man being made in the image of God. In our liturgical language we dropped the reverent "Thou" for the familiar "You." We are building churches in the round so that we might look at each other while we worship rather than looking up to a high and distant altar as the symbol of God's majestic presence. In our snuggling up to God and getting too familiar with him, we have lost the sense of awe, respect, reverence for the greatness of God.

This is not the testimony of the Bible's characters in their experience with God. The Hebrews would not allow the name of God to be spoken by taking out the vowels of his name: YHWH. They gave a substitute name for God: *Adonai,* translated "Lord." God is so great that man is not worthy to speak the holy name of God. Again, when the ark of the covenant was moved to Jerusalem, Uzzah touched the ark lest it fall from the wagon when it went over rough terrain. When he touched the ark, he fell over dead. In the Bible man was not allowed to see God, not even Moses. The most Moses could see was the back of God. To look at the glory of God was like looking at the sun during an eclipse: It burned out your eyes to the point of blindness.

This lack of appreciating the greatness of God has affected our worship. Today the church is experiencing a crisis in worship simply because we no longer have a God worthy of worship, "worth-ship." It is when we have a God of greatness, majesty, and glory that we instinctively fall down before him in worship, awe, and adoration. How much awe is there in the average worship service today other than a child saying, "Aw, do I have to go?"

We fear God not only because of his greatness but because of his power. We have lost this concept of God because modern man has so much power. Why should we be impressed with God's power? We Americans gloried in our military power when we rescued a merchant ship from Cambodia. Brezhnev of Russia called for a new treaty to ban weapons far more powerful, he said, than nuclear weapons. It is said one of our satellites can photograph a pack of cigarettes from a distance of eighty miles in the sky. With all that power, who wants more power, especially from God?

It is hard to describe God's infinite power which makes man's power puny. We see God's power sampled in nature: a hurricane, a tornado, or an earthquake. On Good Friday, 1964, there was an earthquake in Alaska. It was so terrific that mountains fell five feet, and a ridge of mountains moved laterally seven feet. The ocean floor in an area 480 by 178 miles rose fifty feet. This is just the tip of the iceberg of God's power. Because we have forgotten about God's power, we have lost confidence in the power of prayer by which God's power becomes effective. When we appreciated God's power, the hour of prayer was called the hour of power. In the light of God's power, we ask, "Is there anything too hard for God?" God is able to fulfill his promises and to answer our prayers. We may think a human problem or a human need is impossible of solution, but God is able to do the impossible. Prayer is the means of getting God's power applied to our human needs.

Our fear of God is based upon God's holiness. On traditional altars were the words, "Holy, Holy, Holy." These words reminded worshipers of the otherness of God. To be holy is to be different. God is totally different from man. God is absolute purity, absolute goodness, absolute perfection. Man is totally the opposite. This means that man is a sinner and needs to confess and repent. Because God was considered dead, man lost his sense of sin. Menninger felt it necessary to write a book for clergymen, *Whatever Became of Sin?* If God is non-existent, then there is no sin. Man is accountible to no one. He makes up his own morality and whatever he thinks is right is right for him and no one dare challenge or judge him. Sounds very modern and familiar, doesn't it? As a result, we have dropped the custom of going to confession. The Roman Church made a national survey of members over age seventeen and learned that two out of three said they had not gone to confession in the past two months. Non-liturgical Protestants do not even bother to have confession and absolution as parts of their worship services. Why should we confess if we have nothing to confess to a God who has been robbed of his holiness?

Biblical characters gained a sense of sin when they confronted a holy God. At the burning bush, Moses was told to take off his sandals, symbolic of his dirtiness. When Isaiah saw God on a high throne and heard the song, "Holy, Holy, Holy," he fell down and confessed his sins. When Peter realized who Jesus was, he fell on his knees and cried, "Depart from me, Lord, for I am a sinful man." Because we have lost the holiness of God, we no longer fall on our faces and cry, "God, be merciful to me a sinner." The news media reported that prostitutes in Paris took over a church and refused to leave it until their demands were met to stop police harrassment in terms of fines for plying their trade. They were pictured lying on the floor in front of the chancel. They were not crying, "God, be merciful to us sinners" but were defiant and wanted their rights to sin openly and freely! That is characteristic of our times. It is time to recover the holiness of God. Then we will fear his wrath and judgment. We will confess our sins and beg for mercy. Having received mercy, we will have reason to thank and praise him.

The Face of God the Son

In the second place, we see the face of God the Son whom we are to love. Jesus told us to win converts by baptizing them in the name of the Son. God is not only Father but he is also equally God the Son in Jesus Christ. You see, the God as Father we have been considering is far beyond us, totally other from us. God the Father is really incomprehensible and unapproachable. Man needs Jesus as God in a human being. When we know God in Jesus, we not only fear but love him.

We can love him because he reveals God the Father. By his own reason and with his puny mind man cannot comprehend the nature of God. It is like St. Augustine who was trying to understand the Trinity. In a dream he saw a little boy on the seashore trying to empty the ocean into a small hole with a sea shell. He asked the child what he was doing, and the lad answered, "I am just emptying the ocean into this hole." Augustine laughed saying, "You can never do that!" Then God said to him, "Indeed? And you would empty the mysteries of the Infinite God with the little dipper of your thoughts?" Jesus is God in person. He brings God down to man's comprehension. He becomes concrete and specific, a God who can be heard and touched. We need Jesus to reveal God the Father to us, or we would never truly know God.

We love God, too, because Jesus is the mediator between this awesome God and man. God is too great to be approachable. Who can stand in God's holy presence? Who dares to look at God? Who has the right words to say to God? It is utterly impossible for sinful man to get close to God. That is why man needs a mediator, a go-between God in Jesus. Jesus takes our petitions to the Father. Jesus stands as our Advocate when we appear for judgment. Jesus makes all things right between God and man.

Jesus serves as our redeemer. He makes sinners acceptable to God the Father. God is not only love but also justice. When God's laws and will are defied, there is a price to be paid. Justice must be satisfied. In our time we have forgotten there is such a thing as the wrath of God. The wrath of God is the justice of God being applied to sinful man. The very integrity of God forces satisfaction to be made of crimes committed. How can man ever repay God? How can man make it up to God for his many sins? It is impossible. God the Son comes to our rescue. He paid the price of our sins on the cross. Now man is accepted, justified because God the Son died in man's place and made full satisfaction to fulfill the demands of a just God. Here we see the love of God in that while we are sinners Christ died for us. It is out of this love for us that we learn to love God in return.

The Face of God the Spirit

Now we look at the third face of God, the Spirit. If God the Father is unknowable and approachable, and if God the Son has left earth and is seated at the right hand of the Father in glory, where does that leave man in his relation to God? He is as bad off as before Jesus came. If we should stop there, God would be a distant, incomprehensible, and unapproachable God. In that case, woe is man! To answer this need, Jesus promised that God would come to believers as Spirit, the alter-ego of Jesus, the comforter, and advocate.

This means that God is immanent in the person of the Holy Spirit. To have the Spirit is to have God in us, in our hearts, minds, and persons. God is not to be found in nature, only evidence of his reality. God is not to be found in social events or historical acts. We can see only evidence of God. You see, God is a Spirit and only man can have the Spirit. Man is body and soul. The soul is within the body. Within the soul is the Spirit. The soul is like a container for a spirit which may be the good or the bad spirit. When the spirit is bad, we say we are devil-possessed. When we have a good spirit, we have the Holy Spirit. One of the heresies of our day is the idea that God is present in nature, social events, and in all people. The truth is, God is present in the world to the extent that his Spirit is present. Man as a human being does not come with the Holy Spirit. Thus, Jesus taught that a man must be born again, born of the Spirit.

Two men were rushing to catch a plane. One of them knocked down a little boy and his puzzle was scattered on the floor. He stopped to help the boy pick up the pieces and restore the puzzle. The other man was urgent in telling him to come or they would miss the plane. When the puzzle was together, the lad asked, "Mister, are you Jesus?" Today most people would answer, "Yes." The truth is that the man was only a man. He was not Jesus. He was a man with the spirit of Jesus, with the Holy Spirit that made him helpful.

The wonderful good news about this truth of God the Spirit is that God can be closer to us than hands and feet. We do not have to look for God or desire him to come to us. In the person of the Spirit, God is truly with us and in us. It is God in Spirit who works in us to help us, to guide us into truth, to motivate us to do good, and to give us gifts by which we serve God. In 1 Corinthians Paul tells us what those gifts of the Spirit are. In Galatians he lists nine fruits of the Spirit. By virtue of those gifts and fruits of character, you have God in you. You have the Spirit. Speaking in tongues is not the only way to tell whether the Spirit is present. It is far more important to have the Spirit in terms of gifts of service and fruits of virtues than to be able to speak gibberish which may be meaningful to the speaker in tongues but is totally a mystery to all hearers. It is important for us to know and realize that the good we do and the virtues we possess are the work of the Spirit. Only God can make man good, and he does it by the Spirit. This has practical consequences for a society that is saturated with crime and corruption. The only way to gain a better society is to bring people to God that the Spirit might make them good, even like unto God. The ultimate answer to our crime is the birth of the Spirit in the hearts of all men.

After considering the greatness and transcendence of God, do we not come to the same conclusion as Paul did in Romans? When we think of the goodness and power and holiness of God, we are overwhelmed with his majesty. With Paul we sing a doxology: "O the depth of the riches and wisdom and knowledge· of God! How unsearchable are his judgments and how inscrutable are his ways! For who has known the mind of the Lord, or who has been his counselor? Or who has given a gift to him that he might be repaid? For from him and through him and to him are all things. To him be glory forever. Amen." When we think of God as Father, Son, and Holy Spirit, we want to explode and shout with joyous praise: "My God, how wonderful thou art." Today we go home saying the words of Jude: "... to the only God, our Savior through Jesus Christ our Lord, be glory, majesty, dominion, and authority before all time, and now and for ever. Amen."

Can a Christian Go to Hell?
Pentecost II

Not everyone who says to me, "Lord, Lord", shall enter the kingdom of heaven, but he who does the will of my Father who is in heaven. (Matthew 7:21)

If as a Christian you land in heaven, will you be surprised? Once a pastor was invited back by his former congregation to speak for an anniversary celebration. A dear old lady came up to him and said, "And, of course, you know about my dear husband, Albert. Since you left, dear Albert died and has gone to heaven." Since he vaguely remembered Albert as one whose moral life left much to be desired, he replied, "Oh, so Albert died and went to heaven? Well, I must say I'm glad." Since this remark was not too well received, he tried to recover by saying, "What I meant to say was 'I'm sorry!'" This did not help the widow. He tried one more time, "What I really meant to say was, 'I'm surprised!'"

In our text Jesus is saying that if you do not put your faith into practice, you will be surprised to find yourself in hell. Just because you and I are members of a church does not guarantee entrance into heaven. When a new pastor came to town, someone said, "I certainly hope that you're not one of these narrow-minded ministers who think that only the members of their congregation are going to heaven." He replied, "I'm even more narrow-minded than that! I'm pretty sure that some of the members of *my* congregation aren't going to make it!"

There is truth in the Negro spiritual which says, "Everybody talkin' 'bout heab'n ain't goin' dar." In many churches there is a performance gap. We have faith without works, words without deeds, profession without performance. In today's Gospel lesson Jesus tells us that entrance into heaven depends upon putting our faith into practice, upon obedience to God's laws. The passage comes as a conclusion to the Sermon on the Mount. He who hears Jesus' words and does not obey them is like a man who builds his house on sand. He who obeys his words is like a man who builds his house on rock. In the storms of life only the obedient man, built upon the rock of God's will, will be able to remain steady and secure. According to our text, the Christian who does the will of God will go to heaven, and the one content with "Lord, Lord" does not stand a chance.

To Hell You Go!

The word-only Christian, Jesus says, will not go to heaven. "Not every one who says to me "Lord, Lord," shall enter the kingdom of heaven." It is not because Christ wants to be mean and exclude anyone. No, it is the desire of God that every single soul should go to heaven to live with him through eternity. If we do not make it to heaven, it is because we exclude ourselves by our lack of faith. Some of us church members make believe without really believing. We say one thing and do another. Our lives do not correspond to our faith. This makes us hypocrites, actors, make-believers. Some fall on their knees on Sundays and fall upon their neighbors the rest of the week. Our inconsistency can be like the man who wrote forty articles and two booklets on how to spot a bad check artist. Then he was found guilty of having written more than $100,000 worth of hot checks and is now serving a jail term for it.

If we are inconsistent, we are fooling no one but ourselves. Surely, we are not fooling God by making believe that we are genuine followers of the Christ. He sees through the emptiness of our phrases, "Lord, Lord", when we do nothing to serve or obey him. Our church membership may be a false security for some of us. We think that church membership is an automatic ticket to heaven. Our prayers and our praises may be lulling us into a spiritual sleep, the sleep of death. When judgement comes, we may be surprised by being excluded from heaven. Jesus said, "Inasmuch as you have not done it to one of the least of these my brethren you have not done it to me . . . Depart from me, you cursed, into the eternal fire prepared for the devil and his angels; for I was hungry and you gave me no food . . . "In Romans 2 Paul says, "He will render to every man according to his works . . . for those who are factious and do not obey the truth, but obey wickedness, there will be wrath and fury." Our eternal destiny depends not on our words but on our works.

The word-only Christian is excluded from heaven also because he discredits Christianity and the church. At a country crossroads there were only a few buildings: a school, a church, and a country store. The owner of the store was the lay leader of the church. He was so pious that after each sale as he rang up the price on the cash register he would quote a verse of Scripture. When someone bought a loaf of bread, he would say as he rang up the price, "Man shall not live by bread alone." One day a stranger came in to buy a saddle blanket. In the store several old cronies were sitting on barrels, chatting and smoking. They overheard the stranger ask for a blanket. They knew that the store had but one quality of blanket selling for $10.95. The merchant showed him a yellow blanket and said it was $10.95. The man asked if he did not have a better one. The merchant pulled out a blue blanket and said it was $15.95. The customer said he had a fine horse and wanted only the best for him. Did he have a better blanket? The merchant brought out a red one and said the price was $20.95. The sale was completed and the spectators wondered what Bible verse he would now say as he rang up the price. With much dignity, the church leader quoted, "He was a stranger and I took him in."

Can you not imagine the disgust on the part of the other men toward the merchant's church and religion?

They probably said in their hearts:
They're praising God on Sunday.
They'll be all right on Monday.
It's just a little habit they acquired.
Some time ago I had a black student who submitted a sermon entitled, "Damn it, Where Are the Christians?" In anger he told of his poverty and about the conditions in which he grew up. He said, "Damn it, where were the Christians when our floors were covered with wall-to-wall roaches? Damn it, where were the Christians when my father deserted and my mother had nothing to eat for us children? Damn it, where were the Christians when I had to go to a black school with the poorest of teachers?" You see, people who are living in destitute conditions look at affluent church people and become cynical about our profession of love for neighbor.

It is only when we live our faith that others are attracted to the church. There was a missionary who addressed a group of Hindu women. While he was talking, one left but soon returned and listened with greater intensity. After the meeting, he asked her why she left. She explained, "I was so interested in the wonderful things you were saying about Christ that I wanted to ask your servant if you live like you teach. He said that you did and I came back to hear more about your Jesus."

This word-only type of Christianity excludes us from heaven because it really offends God. In Isaiah God says, "I cannot endure iniquity and solemn assembly. Your new moons and your appointed feasts my soul hates . . . even though you make many prayers, I will not listen." Luther once said "Perhaps God would rather hear the cries of the ungodly then the hallelujahs of the pious."

Though we are pious and say our prayers, though we go regularly to church and sing our alleluias, though we faithfully place even a tithe on the offering plate, and stop there without any effort being made to put faith into practice, God cannot stand us. He is hurt and offended and grieved no end. He detests make-believe and artificiality. You will recall that Cain's prayers were not heard because his heart at the time was full of hatred for his brother, Abel. In the Sermon on the Mount Jesus said that only the pure in heart see God. When Jesus found a fig tree that was supposed to have fruit and did not have any, he cursed it for its fruitlessness. This is a parable of what we can expect for our lack of putting our religion into life. Our record in putting faith into practice is not good and leaves much to be desired. Many times we church people do not act like children of God. We are more like wolves than sheep.

Will we as nominal Christians have to face the judgment of exclusion because of our lack of Christian morality? Pierre von Paassen in his book *Days of our Years*, tells of a little hunchback, Ugolin, who lived in a small French village. He had a hard time because he was a monstrous looking creature. Children would not play with him. One night some drinking men starting making fun of him. They kicked him, spit on him, tore off his clothes, and finally left him in a pool of blood. Later that night the local priest found him, took him home, washed him, and put him to bed. The next day while the priest was conducting mass, Ugolin went to the river and drowned himself. When his sister found it out, she committed suicide. Though they were suicides, the priest planned a double funeral in the church, for he said, "Those children were not suicides. They have been murdered by society without mercy." The day came for the funeral and the priest went to the pulpit. While looking at every one, he waited to begin the sermon. He began, "Christians! When the Lord of Life and of Death shall ask me on the Day of Judgment, 'Pastor, where are your sheep.' I will not answer him. On the third time he will ask, 'Pastor . . . where . . . are . . . your sheep?' I will hang my head in shame and I will answer, 'They were not sheep, Lord . . . they were a pack of wolves!' "

Can the Will of God Be Done?

Now we have seen that our text of Jesus' words tells us who will not go to heaven even if they are "Christians" who say, "Lord, Lord." The text goes on to tell us what Christians will enter the kingdom of God: "But he who does the will of my Father in heaven." It is not the word-only Christian but the work-Christian that goes to heaven. It is the believer who puts his faith into action. It is the Christian who obeys the commands of God and reaps his blessing in heaven. Is this not a hard saying? Who then can enter the Kingdom, for who really practices his Christianity as he should? How can we church members do the will of God as Jesus demands?

It can be done not by doing but by being a Christian. A youth once asked a friend, "What can I do, man?" the other replied, "Don't do, man. Be." Many of us make the mistake of thinking that we can obey the Lord's commands by getting busy and trying harder and harder to shape up to what God expects of us. This is nothing more than self-salvation, works-righteousness. We think that we can get to heaven on our own efforts in moral endeavor. There is the big mistake. It is not doing but being. Out of being comes the doing. We will never be able to obey the will of God until we first become true and genuine Christians. We must first be godly before we can act in a godly manner. This points us to the core of one's being, the heart, the nature of a person. Jesus taught that a good tree will produce good fruit and a bad tree will produce like fruit. The problem is not in the fruit but in the condition of the tree that produces the fruit. The reason we do nothing or the wrong things is due to the fact that our hearts are not right. We are not rooted and grounded in Christ. We act according to what we are. During slavery days, northern visitors in New Orleans were watching slaves working spiritlessly and dragging themselves along. But one, in striking contrast, worked with his head erect and with an unbroken spirit.

Someone asked, "Who is that fellow? Is he the straw boss or the owner of the slaves?" "No," came the reply, "That fellow just can't get it out of his head that he is the son of a king." Because he was a prince, he acted like a prince even in slavery.

If we church members are not living and serving as we should, it means that we are in need of a change of heart. We need to be converted to Christ. We need to be reborn in the Spirit. If we have been born again, we need a new birth of the Spirit with a deeper and closer relationship with Christ. This calls for a oneness in Christ. Our problem may be that we, the branches, are not in the vine, Christ. If we were one in Christ, good works would flow naturally and spontaneously from this relationship. Our good deeds would result as naturally as fruit on a tree. Our practical service to others would flow from us as water comes from a fountain. There is no force connected with it. Goodness flows from a good heart. The question then, is, "Brother, how is your heart?"

Obedience, moreover, to the will of God is not in works but in faith. That sounds contradictory, doesn't it? We have just been saying that faith without works can throw you into hell. Now we are saying that obedience to God's commands is not in the works of obedience but in faith in Christ. This is really not contradictory. It is the biblical truth. Faith and works are inseparable. But faith precedes works. Luther was right when he said that faith and works cannot be separated any more than light and heat can be separated from a fire. Works are the expression of faith. If we are interested in doing good works, if we want to be obedient to God's will then our great need is for faith. For true faith always expresses itself. Faith without an outlet is no faith at all.

To get faith, we need more than a shallow "belief." About ninety-five percent of the American people claim they believe in God but not all these have faith. A college coed once said, "Sure I believe in God; I'm just not nuts about him." That kind of faith will not produce good deeds or obey God's commands. The faith that results in practice is a faith of a David when he goes out to fight the giant, Goliath. He put his whole trust in God and the result was a fearless facing of the giant. Gideon had a faith that obeyed God's orders to defeat an army of tens of thousands with a handful of three hundred men. The truth is that we do or give according to what we believe in. During the 1976 presidential election, people voted for Carter because they believed in him. Donors give millions to higher education because they believe in our colleges. A man with a salary of $25,000 and a family of five felt called to the ministry. He sold his house, moved his family to a seminary, and took a small church with a salary of $5,000. Why did he do this "crazy" thing? He did it because he believed that he was called to preach. He believed that God wanted him to serve in this way. He was sure that the church and the gospel had the answer to the world's needs. It is faith — real faith — that makes us do things such as obeying God's will. So, the problem we face is not less faith but a faith that is so deep that we would even die for it.

You and I can get to heaven by doing the will of the Father if we will not love man but love God. That sounds foolish, too, doesn't it? It seems we have been talking about loving our neighbor by feeding the hungry, giving drink to the thirsty, and so on. That is true, but we forget what will make us love our fellowmen. It is not a matter of deciding to love people but to love God. Love of God must come first. The first commandment, Jesus said, is to love God with your whole person, and then you love your neighbor, the second commandment. The reason we love God before we love our fellowmen is that God first loves us and makes it possible for us to love each other. "We love him because he first loved us." Our love is a response to the love of God experienced in Christ. First there is the vertical dimension of love —

love of God in response to God's prior love. Then there is the horizontal dimension of love — love for each other as a response to our love for God.

If God loves us, how can we in return love God? We love God by loving our fellow humans. Some years ago *Life* magazine took a picture of a girl seated between two boys on a wall with their backs to the camera. The one boy had his arm around the girl while at the same time the girl held hands with the other boy behind their backs. This is the position of a true Christian. He first loves God and God has his arms around him, but at the same time his arms go out to those next to him. The caption of the picture was "Love is a backhanded thing." Yes, our love for our fellowmen is not a direct or natural love. It comes through the back door. Many people are not worth loving. Many are not loveable. Christians do not love their fellowmen because they are worthy of love. We love people because we first love God and his Christ. We see Christ in those who need our love.

While we are concerned about obeying the will of God to love all men, our need is not to go out to love people but first to learn to love God. Our prayer needs to be in the words of a hymn, "More love to thee, O Christ . . . more love to thee."

There is a tombstone at Hard Labor Creek State Park which has this inscription: "Noell Nelson, died 1849. He was a member of the Protestant Church and we hope died a Christian." A member of a church who is not a Christian may be one who is content to say only "Lord, Lord." To him the gates of heaven are closed. The church member who does the will of the Father enters the Kingdom. There is no need to hope he will go to heaven. He is there. You and I can have the same assurance if we are both a word and a work Christian.

Sinner to Saint
Pentecost III

As Jesus passed on from there, he saw a man called Matthew sitting at the tax office; and he said to him, "Follow me". And he rose and followed him. (Matthew 9:9)

"You've come a long way, Baby" is an expression used by a popular cigarette commercial. You are shown a 19th century girl who is hiding her smoking with embarrassment. In contrast there is a 20th century girl openly, proudly smoking a cigarette. Indeed, women smokers have come a long way from public displeasure to acceptance.

To become a saint, a sinner comes a long way, too. In June, 1977, the first American male became a saint by Roman Catholic canonization. John Neumann came to this country as an immigrant from Bohemia. He is know for his work of helping immigrants to this country, establishing the Roman Catholic school system in America, and serving as bishop of Philadelphia for eight years prior to his death in 1860. After more than a century, Neumann will be made a saint.

Our text is a one-verse biography of a man who came a long way from sinner to saint — Matthew. He was a tax collector, a publican who in that day was considered a super-sinner because he was a traitor to his country by collecting taxes from the Jews to support the Roman government. Jesus came to him where he was and made him an apostle. Now the world knows him as Saint Matthew. It was a long way for Matthew, too, from being a sinner to becoming a saint.

Do you think it is possible for you and me to become a saint? If it is possible, it will be a long way, for we have much ground to cover. Yet, it is possilbe. Years ago there was a man in the west who was caught stealing sheep. They branded him on the forehead with the letters ST, "sheep thief." Later his life changed and he became a model for all. People forgot that ST stood for "sheep thief" and thought it symbolized "saint." This is what Jesus wants to happen in every person's life, including yours and mine. He associated with sinners, had dinner with them, and once explained to his enemies that he came to call sinners that they might become saints of God. How can we cover the long distance from sinner to saint? In our text we have an example in Matthew. If we follow him, we, too, can come a long way.

Confronted by Christ

The journey from sinner to saint begins when Christ confronts you. This happened with Matthew. Our text says, "As Jesus passed on from there, he saw a man called Matthew sitting at the tax office . . ." Jesus came into his office, took a chair opposite his desk, and confronted Matthew face to face, eye to eye, and heart to heart. There was no dodging Jesus. There he was, right in front of him. It was a man-to-man confrontation, and something had to happen.

Probably you are saying that you wish you could have such a confrontation with Jesus right now. You may be saying, "Oh, if Jesus would only come to my office in the morning and have a conversation with me!" or "If Jesus would only come to my kitchen and sit down across from me at the kitchen table!" How wonderful that would be! There are so many things we would like to ask him. We need his guidance for the problems that we face.

Of course, we know that this is not possible today as it was in the time of Matthew. Jesus is no longer physically on earth. Now he is a spiritual presence and not a material reality. While this is true, it is still possible to get to know Jesus as though he were physically in the same room with us. Physical proximity does not necessarily mean that we get to know a person. Genesis says that Abraham "knew" Sarah and she conceived and bore a son. To know in the Bible means a close, intimate personal relationship. The Germans have two words for knowing. One is *wissen*, meaning to know things or facts. The other is *kennen*, meaning to know people. We can know Jesus more intimately today than some who were present with him physically. When Jesus was with a crowd during the days of John the Baptizer, John said that there was one who stood among them they did not know. Pilate physically and privately confronted Jesus when he was on trial, but Pilate never knew the real Jesus, for he asked, "Are you the king of the Jews?" One of his disciples, Philip, was with him for three years, but still did not know him. Philip said, "Show us the Father, and we shall be satisfied." Jesus replied, "Have I been with you so long, and yet you do not know me, Philip?" So often we think of Jesus as being 2,000 years away from us as a figure of ancient history similar to Plato or Caesar or Alexander the Great. We should not think of history in its linear form in terms of a straight line from Jesus to us, 2,000 years' distance. Think of Jesus as the hub of history, and each century as a spoke. In that concept, we in the 20th century can be as close to Jesus as those in the 1st century. Thus, we can know Jesus personally, truly through faith. He can confront us today as he confronted Matthew.

How does Jesus confront us today since he is not physically present? He can confront us in the Word of God. When we read or hear the Word read or preached, Christ confronts us with his presence, for the Scriptures testify of him. This happened to Augustine who, while meditating in his garden, heard the words, *Teke lege*, "take and read." He went to an open Bible and read, "Put on the Lord Jesus Christ . . .", and Christ became a reality to him. John Wesley was confronted by Christ as he listened to one reading Luther's preface to the book of

Romans and for the first time he felt that Christ was really his Savior. When a pastor or other member of the church comes to you and asks you to do something for the church or to speak to you about your relationship with Christ, it is Christ in him who confronts you. Christ may confront you in and through a need. It may be a neighbor in poverty. It could be a hungry child crying for help. It could be a broken-hearted office colleague.

One thing is sure. Every person who has begun his mission from sinner to saint has had a real, personal confrontation with Christ. It may have come in different ways, but it always takes place. For Paul it happened on the Damascus road. For Augustine it was a voice. St. Francis met Christ at a wayside shrine where as he was looking at a crucifix; he heard Christ say, "Sell all and give to the poor and come and follow me." Martin Luther confronted Christ as he prepared his university lectures, particularly when he read the words, "The just shall live by faith." Wesley found Christ in a prayer meeting on Aldersgate Street. One after the other confronted Christ until we come to our times when Billy Graham confronted Christ while attending a tent revival in Charlotte, N.C., conducted by Mordecai Hamm.

What was true for these must be the case with you and me if you want to go from sinner to saint. Our problem is we know so much about Jesus but we do not really know him. We read about him in the Bible. We hear sermons about his life. But, all of this has been formal and objective. For many Christ has never become a personal reality as he was to Matthew in the tax office. It is like a certain bachelor professor who had a friend, an artist. One day he went into his studio and saw a magnificent portrait of a lovely lady. He could not help admiring the painting. The professor asked if he could take it and hang it in his apartment. His friend suggested that maybe he might want to go one better and meet the lady. The bachelor at the time was not interested. Later, however, almost by accident he did meet the lady and in due course they were married. Then the lady moved into the apartment where her portrait was hung. Before the wedding, the lady was just a painting — objective, formal, something to look at and admire. Now she was one to know and love. How many of us have a picture of Jesus hanging on the wall of our homes or offices? Could Jesus be just someone who looks good and one whom we admire? For us to confront Christ, he must come off the wall, step out of the picture and into our hearts where we might know him truly.

Called By Christ

The first milestone in the journey from sinner to saint is to be confronted by Christ. But that is not enough — just getting to know him. Matthew went another mile in his trip from sinner to saint. Our text says, "As Jesus passed on from there, he saw a man called Matthew sitting at the tax office; and he said to him, 'Follow me.' " It is not enough to be confronted by Christ; we must be called by Christ.

We often talk about being called to be Christians. Pastors are supposed to be called to preach. The Disciples were called to follow Jesus. What do we mean when we say "call"? Often we use the word, "call," when we refer to sleep. When we are in a hotel or motel and need to catch a plane or keep an appointment, we usually, before retiring, call the main desk and ask to be called at a certain hour. Our mothers used to call us to get up for school or work. A call may imply that we are asleep and need to get awake.

Many Christians are asleep spiritually. St. Francis felt it was his mission in life to awaken spiritually asleep people. This can be the case with church people who have been Christians since infant baptism. They have been raised in Christian homes, attended church school since nursery days, and have been worshiping faithfully for years. By this time religion has become routine and matter-of-fact. They have never awakened to who they are and what they ought to be doing with their lives. Isn't it a tragedy to be a Christian and not know it? There is a legend about a little fish who overheard fishermen say that a fish needed water to live. The little fish became worried and started hunting for water. He swam from creek to river to the seven seas. One time he met a big, old fish who saw how worried the little fish was and asked what the trouble was. The little fish explained that he was looking for water because he heard the fishermen say that a fish cannot live without water. The big fish laughed and said, "O little fish, why are you worried? Don't you know that you are in the water all the time?" It is time for us who have been on the church rolls from infancy to wake up and realize whose we are. Then we will know who we are and in whom we have our being. We need to awaken to the fact that we are children of God by grace through baptism, and as children of God we have a mission in life.

It may also be true that the whole church today is asleep, and needs to be called by Christ. Sleep, you know, can be used as an escape from our responsibilities. We can use sleep to dodge God's call to serve. Jonah used this method. He got on a boat to avoid preaching to Nineveh, and during a severe storm he was found fast asleep in the hold of the ship. How could anyone sleep during a storm? Sleep is a good way of getting rid of an unpleasant world. Isn't that why some people take sleeping pills and tranquillizers to avoid the unpleasantness of vexatious problems of life? Sleep may also be a symptom of indifference. This was the case with the three Disciples in Gethsemane. Jesus asked them to pray for him while he prayed about the cross. When he came back to them, he found them asleep and asked, "Can you not watch with me one hour?" When your best friend is sweating blood amd making a life-or-death decision, can you really be relaxed enough to sleep if you really are concerned about your friend? Sleep is a company of Christians was crossing the desert and I loosed the lions on them and all were lost." The devil replied, "What good was that? Their bodies were lost but their souls were saved. I want their souls." Another little devil reported that a company of Christians was crossing the sea. He sent strong winds and caused the ship to go on the rocks and all were lost. Satan again said that was nothing because though their bodies were lost, he wanted their souls. A third gave his report that after years of trying he finally managed to put the church to sleep. At this the corridors of hell rang with the shouts of malignant triumph.

Christ calls a man out of his spiritual slumber to follow him in service. He said to Matthew, "Follow me." Today Christians likewise are called to serve both in the world and in the church. The world is crying out to us Christians for help. People are in trouble and are sounding an SOS; shall we not hear? The world is like a drowning person, and with all his might, he is crying, "Help, help, help!" Shall we not respond? The call of Christ to serve may come from some need that exists. That is how Paul understood Christ's call to serve in Macedonia. He had a vision of a man saying, "Come to Macedonia and help us." Note that the call did not come from a voice in the sky. No angel came asking help for Macedonia. The call came from the lips of a human being.

Christ calls us to serve in the church. Some are called to full-time service in and through the church. Others are called to do part-time work. Pastors, teachers, musicians, cooks, nursery workers, ushers, visitors, and helpers of all kinds are called to serve Christ through the church. But some are called to full-time service to Christ in the world. This is the usual role of the laity. Each Christian should have a vocation, a calling. He is called to be a carpenter, or a secretary, or a salesman, or plumber, or a pilot, or a politician. The list is almost endless. A true Christian is called to go into the world and serve Christ according to the call and his talents. This is what Christ wants you to do with your life. With this sense of vocation you become a minister of God, a priest of Christ. Then a person's life has meaning and purpose. You are not merely working for wages, or to make a living. You are out there day after day glorifying God through his service.

Changed by Christ

You and I have a long way to go from sinner to saint. The journey is not complete until we go another mile in our spiritual pilgrimage. We see this final step in Matthew. "As Jesus passed on from there, he saw a man called Matthew sitting at the tax office; and he said to him, 'Follow me.' And he rose and followed him." Here we see that it is not enough to be confronted by Christ, nor to be called by Christ, but to be changed by Christ. After that visit, Matthew was never the same again. He was a changed person. He turned from a publican to a preacher, from a tax collector to a soul gatherer, from a sinner to a saint.

The truth is that life is never the same again when Christ comes into your life. When he confronts and calls you, you face that one moment of decision. Are you for him or against him? Will you follow — yes or no? You have to make a decision. You have to be on one side or the other. At a formal wedding, an usher usually asks, "Friend of the bride or the groom?" Then he seats the party on the appropriate side of the church. An usher once asked a lady, "Friend of the bride or the groom?" She replied, "Both." He explained, "I am sorry, lady. They did not tell me where to seat neutrals!" That is the way it is with Christ. There are no neutrals. If you make an affirmative decision, your life is radically changed. "He rose and followed him."

This is based on the assumption that life can be changed. It is a fact that you can change and that Christ has the power to change your life. A criminal can become Christlike. Blackie spent thirty years in jail. One Easter he presented himself for baptism, for he found Christ. He explained the change in him, "I've tried everything else. Nothing works. I don't have all the answers, but I have decided to put my chips on Jesus." In recent times Charles Colson, author of *Born Again*, was deeply involved in the Watergate scandal. It was said he was so ruthless that to accomplish his goal he would run over even his grandmother. Now he tells about the love of God that turned him around. Eldridge Cleaver, leader of the Black Panthers who were dedicated to the violent overthrow of our government, came back to America, turned himself in to the FBI, and expressed an entirely different opinion of America. What happened to him? In recent months he was introduced to Christ and is now a follower of him.

What can cause this change? It is the power of the Word, of Jesus Christ. A missionary tells of celebrating a Communion service attended by two tribes who were seated in perfect harmony. Less than a generation ago, the warriors of both tribes dipped their spears in each other's blood, stole each other's wives, burned their homes, and destroyed their crops. Then Christ was brought to their villages, and now they fellowship around the table of Christ. It gets down to simply this: you and I do not have to be the way we are. We can change from someone ugly to a person beautiful. We can be different. We shall be changed to the degree that we allow Christ to come into our lives.

You may ask just what is the nature of that change that Christ causes. It is essentially an internal rather than an external change. There may be a visible change after the internal change in the heart. Some think that being a Christian demands certain outward changes such as the non-wearing of jewelry, cutting one's hair, playing cards, or going to dances. Some years ago a farmer went to a big city and stepped into a hotel lobby where there was an elevator. He watched how people walked into the elevator, doors closed, and then an indicator like a hand of a clock pointed to the number of the floor where the elevator was. He noticed how people got on the elevator and shortly they stepped off it. He saw an overweight woman get on and soon there stepped off the same elevator a slender lady. Seeing that, he took off his hat, scratched his head, and was heard to say to himself, "I wish I had brought Margie with me. She needs that treatment." It is not an external change that is necessarily made, but an internal one: a new spirit, a change of attitude, love instead of hatred. There is an about-face in values.

The change that Christ makes in our lives is not superficial but radical. It is not a matter of filling up pot-holes in the road but rebuilding the road. It is not a matter of putting band-aids on a cut here and there, but it involves the whole sickness. Zeke, a mountaineer, went to a revival and was "converted." Later his wife was asked if she noticed any change in Zeke since he supposedly got religion. She said, "Well, before he carried his jug of whiskey on his shoulder when he walked down town, but now he caries it under his coat." This is not the kind of change Christ makes in our lives. This change goes to the very depths of our beings. There is a radical change of heart. The changed person is a new being in Christ.

The change may not be sudden, but there may be a slow, gradual change as the years go by in response to fellowship with Christ. The change may take place so quietly that the person himself does not know he is changing. Of course, some people are changed immediately. That was the experience of St. Paul on the Damascus road. In Max Beerbohm's *Happy Hypocrite* a wicked man wore a mask of a saint in order to woo a saintly woman he loved. Years later a woman he had cast off discovered his trick and challenged him to take off his mask in front of his sweetheart that she might know the truth about him. He did it only to find that behind the mask of a saint there was his true face which had become that of a saint. As we live for Christ, as we daily practice doing good, as we spend time constantly with Christ, eventually and gradually we become like Christ, a changed person.

But, this change will not take place until, like Matthew, we leave all and follow Jesus. It calls for complete and total surrender to Christ. Dwight L. Moody once heard a Christian teacher, Henry Varley, say to a group, "The world has yet to see what God can do with and for and through and in a man who is fully and wholly consecrated to him." While in church that night, listening to Spurgeon, Moody decided, "I will try my utmost to be that man." Out of that complete commitment came the great evangelist, Moody. The same can be the case with you. You will never know what good God can do with your life until you surrender it to him now.

We do not have to ask who a sinner is, because each of us knows himself. But, what is a saint? He is one who, like a stained glass window, lets the light of Christ shine through him. He does this because Christ lives in him and he in Christ. Luther once said, "If you should knock on my heart and ask, 'Who lives there?' I would not say, 'Martin Luther lives there.' Rather I would say, 'Jesus Christ lives there.' " When you can say that, you have gone from sinner to saint!

Converting the Converted
Pentecost IV

These twelve Jesus sent out, charging them, "Go nowhere among the Gentiles, and enter no town of the Samaritans, but go rather to the lost sheep of the house of Israel. And preach as you go, saying, 'The Kingdom of heaven is at hand.' " (Matthew 10:5-7)

Have you ever wondered why, with a church on almost every corner in America, so much evil abounds? In a country with approximately 120 million church members, 98 million gamble, costing $5.1 billion per year. In a land where seventy-one percent of the population claims to belong to a church, more than 20,000 people are murdered every year. In a so-called Christian nation how do you account for the fact that each year employees steal $50 billion worth of goods from their employers? Is there not something out of kilter when some years ago the city of Charlotte, N.C. had the dubious honor of having, on a per capita basis, the highest number of churches in America, but also the highest crime rate?

Does it mean that the church needs to be converted before she can convert others? What if the salt has lost its saltness? Can the blind lead the blind? Can the foolish make men wise? If the church has no light, can she dispel the darkness of the world? Can a lost person find the lost? Can we make others Christian when we are Christians only in name? It doesn't make sense, does it? What is wrong with the church? Should she not have some influence to make this a better country? Why doesn't the church make a good society?

This is the issue with which we are confronted in today's Gospel lesson. It is perhaps shocking to some of you to hear, in our text, Jesus sending out his Disciples to preach, teach, and heal only the Jews. He expressly commanded them not to go to the Samaritans or to any other people — "Go nowhere among the Gentiles." At the end of his mission Jesus gives as his final commission, "Go therefore and make disciples of all nations . . . Go into all the world and preach the gospel to the whole creation." But now, at this stage of the game, Jesus prohibits them from giving the good news to anyone except Jews. Our first lesson for this Sunday helps us to understand why he said this. God says he chose the Jews to be a special people to him that through Israel the whole world would be blessed and come to God. God said that the Jews were to be a kingdom of priests and a holy nation. Thus, Jesus feels it is necessary for Israel to become truly Christian before it can evangelize the nations.

If we put this principle down into today's church and world, we can see that Jesus' command is still true. Today the church is God's people, a priesthood of believers, a holy nation. Through the ministry of the church the world is to be brought to God for reconciliation. How can the church do this unless she is first of all solidly and intimately in the Christian faith? Is it not true what someone has said that the church is today's greatest mission field? Jesus is saying to us that the church must first be converted before she can convert the world. Since the church is supposed to be converted, we face the paradoxical situation of the converted converting the converted!

Christians Need Conversion

Why must this be so? For one thing, church members *need* to be converted. Is it true that the church is a field for evangelism? Are we Christians in name only? Are we only hearers of the Word and not doers? Are we long on confession and short on consecration?

If we look at ourselves as members of the church, we see that, in general, we must give an affirmative answer to these questions. Some of us can be religious without being Christian. You know, Paul was at one time a very religious person. He deeply believed in God, tried with all his might to obey the sacred Law, faithfully attended every synagogue service and went regularly to the temple, and volunteered to wipe out the heretics, the Christians of his day. He was pious and strict. He kept the ceremonial law down to the last letter. It was only when he was on the road to Damascus to persecute Christians that he became a Christian. Likewise, many of us in church are deeply religious people. We worship regularly, we pay our tithes, we may volunteer our services, and we often spend some of our time in church functions. We pray almost daily and we might even read the Bible occasionally. Have we become Christians or are we content just to be religious? We can be narrow legalists and proud pietists but not Christian in heart. In the poem, *John Brown's Body*, a sea captain is engaged in the slave trade and prays devoutly every day without any feeling of guilt about his business. John Browning, while governor of Hong Kong, encouraged the opium traffic but yet wrote the popular hymn, "In the Cross of Christ I Glory".

Many church members may not have had a conscious conversion to Christ. Christ has not become a reality to them, and for that reason need to be converted again. Leslie Weatherhead once estimated that ninety percent of church-going people have no vital experience of Christ and have no sense of spiritual power. Could this be true in our congregation? If so, is this not a serious situation? No wonder the world is in the condition it is! How can this be so? It may be due to the fact that most of us were baptized as infants. As in my own case, I was baptized on the thirteenth day after my birth. What can a two weeks' old baby know or understand about a great spiritual experience that baptism involves? This is normal and a child cannot be expected to be aware of his baptism. However, the child upon reaching proper age usually responds to his baptism at the time of Confirmation. At this time he is to know what he is doing, what Christ means to him, and makes a conscious declaration of faith and fidelity to Christ. That is fine in theory, but how many youth between ages twelve and fifteen really understood what they were doing at their Confirmation? Some were confirmed because their friends were going to be confirmed. Some did it because it was a family custom. Even if some were confirmed on their own desire, how many youth of this age can comprehend the deep spiritual experience of Christ? This problem has been accentuated by the recent soft-pedalling of Confirmation in the Lutheran church. In some churches Confirmation is optional and the youth can get around to it when they feel the urge while in the meantime they may take Holy Communion without a public declaration of their faith in Christ.

The need for converting Christians is shown by the great divorce between what we confess as our faith and our execution of it in daily life. As the Government had its scandal in Watergate, the church has its scandals, too. Sin abounds in the church as elsewhere. Take some recent cases of inconsistent Christian living. A French Roman Catholic bishop, as reported by the news media, dies of a heart attack while visiting a prostitute. An outstanding Episcopalian minister tells the press that he is a practicing homosexual. The pastor of a large Protestant church in Florida was compelled to resign because he was accused of embezzling $70,000. This kind of behavior as church members is not only the case with leaders but with the average churchman. A lay leader was in a restaurant one day. The waitress was slow and clumsy because she was new on the job. Suddenly he slapped his hand on the table and snapped, "Damn it, girl! Hurry up with that order! I haven't got all day!" Isn't patience one of the gifts of the Holy Spirit?

The need for conversion is seen in the areas of social concern that have not yet been touched by the gospel.

Take the area of race relations. In Bennett's book, *Before the Mayflower*, members of a Presbyterian church in 1767 bought two slave women. They and their descendants were hired out and the money was used to pay the pastor. In sixty-eight years the number grew to seventy slaves who were sold in 1835 and the money was reinvested. The church considered it a very lucrative religious enterprise. Granted, we have come as a church a long way since then, but we are still unchristian in some cases. Jimmy Carter's church in Plains, Georgia, refused to accept blacks until national prominence of the case made the church change the rule to keep from embarrassing the newly-elected president. Last year a class of black students in the University of Alabama went to a white church holding a revival at the time to study and observe what happens at a revival. The group was turned away and moved off the church's property. A woman with two brothers in the ministry boasted during a dinner, with two other ministers present, that her church in Atlanta has not allowed a black person to enter the church for sixteen years by posting ushers at each door to keep them out.

The tragedy of it all is a diminishing sense of sin among church people. This is indicated in many churches where confession of sin and absolution are not in the order of service. In those churches where confession is a part of the liturgy, the new liturgies make confession optional. No longer do we as church people come to the house of God to confront a holy God and fall on our knees begging, "Be merciful to me, a sinner." Dr. Menninger in his book rightly asks, "Whatever became of sin?" A pastor's wife troubled with nerves went to her doctor who told her, "Don't think of yourself as guilty. Just consider yourself human." Now she did not have to worry about her sins. She accepted her life-style as just an expression of being human. For many, wrong-doing is not a sin, only a sickness. The point is if we of the church are as sinful as people in the world, how can we help the world to be virtuous in all its dealings? If the church does not exhibit a higher quality of life, we are all lost and hopeless. Can't you see, therefore, why Jesus ordered his Disciples to begin their work with their own people before going out to the world?

Conversion Is a Process

In our text Jesus sends us out to our own people, to the church and not to the world. "Go to the lost sheep of the house of Israel." The church is the new Israel. Before the church can go to the world with the gospel calling men to repentance and faith in Christ, the church must first repent and believe. That is why there must be a converting of the converted. It is necessary because, in the second place, conversion is a process.

We usually think of conversion as a once-in-a-lifetime experience. Then we are supposed to be completely changed and totally in Christ. This may happen as it obviously occurred in St. Paul's life. There are unusual cases such as his, but it is not the norm. Conversion is a process of a lifelong turning to Christ. If this is the case, then church members are always in the condition of turning from Satan to Christ, and the process ends only with death. Becoming a full Christian is being a Christian little by little, bit by bit, attitude by attitude, area of life by area. According to this, it is possible for a Christian to say that there never was a time when he did not know himself as a Christian. One can be born one day and the next day can be baptized into Christ. By that baptism God adopted the child as his own, accepted him as a member of the Kingdom, and sent the Holy Spirit to cause a new birth. From this time forth, the person is becoming a Christian.

We might think of becoming a Christian in terms of turning a globe around. You want to turn it completely around, 180 degrees. The turn does not take place instantaneously. It turns little by little, degree by degree until one day it is completely turned around. Consider it in terms of a highway. Suppose you wanted to go from Atlanta to New York. You begin by getting on Interstate 85 and you head north. You go mile after mile, mile after mile. Each mile gets you closer to your destination, but one particular mile does not say that you have arrived. Each day may be considered a mile in going toward the goal of arriving in Christ, the Way. Or, you might think of conversion to Christ in terms of birth, a figure used by Jesus. When a child is born, he is not fully a person. Birth merely means the beginning of a process of growth until eventual adulthood. It takes years of feeding, exercising, and nurturing until you are fully grown.

Apply this to your life in Christ. The beginning of your Christian life is your baptism. Here the turn toward Christ took place. Here was the time of the second birth. Here you started on the highway that leads to God. You were born into a Christian home where your faith was nurtured. Your parents taught you to pray, told you about God, read the Bible to you, and took you with them to church. The day came when you were mature enough to declare your own faith in Christ. Your faith was publicly confirmed. Here was a milestone in your life. But, you are still on the way to oneness in Christ. The end of your journey is not Confirmation. The process of conversion must continue.

Each time you come to church for worship, you will be going a notch higher toward Christ. In worship you are confronted with the Word as it is read and preached. You hear of God's love and you are moved to respond to his love. The service near the end gives you an opportunity to rededicate yourself and to give yourself again more fully then ever. It is called in the liturgy the "offertory," the offering of one's self anew in Christ. Sunday after Sunday there is the opportunity to get closer to Christ. Even a deeper experience involving a closer walk with God can take place when you come to the Holy Communion. In a concrete way Jesus comes to you in the form of bread and wine, the body and blood of Christ. To prepare, you confessed your sin, truly repented, and came forward to be assured of forgiveness. As you knelt at the altar rail, Christ came to you personally in the person of the pastor. You heard the words of Jesus, "Take, eat." This intimate and personal experience with Christ in the Communion may have meant a leap forward in being one with him.

Throughout your life there are special occasions that are most meaningful in becoming a better Christian. It may be in reading the Bible that Christ came very close to you. The notorious sinner, Augustine, found Christ by reading the Bible. The greatest preacher of the 18th century, Jonathan Edwards, was reading his Bible and felt Christ's call to enter the ministry. If you want to grow close to Christ, you don't want to neglect the daily reading of the Word. Christ may come to you, also, in a fresh way by just looking at a picture. This happened to Count Zinzendorf who was at the time a nominal Christian. He saw a large painting of the crucifixion with the words at the bottom, "This I have done for thee. What have you done for me?" This moved him so mightily that he gave his life to Christ and became the fearless and energetic leader of the Moravians. It can be music that will bring you closer to Christ, maybe Handel's *Messiah* or Bach's *Passion According to St. Matthew*. The reading of a book might do it, too. John Wesley was converted when he listened to the reading of Luther's Preface to Romans; His brother, Charles, had a similar experience when he read Luther's Preface to Galatians. These two brothers, through preaching, writing, and hymnody, were responsible for the great movement of revitalized Christianity institutionalized in the Methodist church.

Partners in Conversion

"Converting the converted" — how can the converted convert the converted? This seems like double-talk, but the truth is that God uses the converted to convert "the converted" in the church. In his mercy God uses Christians as partners in converting. This is the third reason for saying that the first mission of the church is to the church rather than to the world. Let us be sure of the fact that God is the author of a conversion. God comes to us in Christ. He takes the initiative. He seeks man, not the other way!

How does God through Christ bring man to repentance and faith? He uses people like you and me. Peter was brought to Christ through his brother Andrew, and thus Andrew is known as the first Christian evangelist. Andrew first found Christ and then brought Peter. Philip was responsible for bringing Nathanael. After Jesus spoke to the Samaritan woman at the well, she went back to her townsmen and told them about Jesus. When they found Jesus, they said to her, "It is no longer because of your words that we believe, for we have heard for ourselves, and we know that this is indeed the Savior of the world." In Paul's case, God used Ananias to bring Paul into the fold. Ananias was sent to Paul to baptize him. Repeatedly God uses someone to speak, contact, and to baptize a person into the Christian faith.

It is generally the case that a person comes to Christ through another person. God needs you to bring others to Christ. You are his instrument. His midwife, to cause people to be born again of the Spirit. Think of your own Christian life and how you came into the Christian faith. If it were not for your parents, you would not probably be in the church today. When you were an infant, they brought you to the baptismal font to be made a Christian. Through the years they nurtured that faith through nursery, kindergarten, primary, and junior ages. They read the Bible stories and knelt with you beside the bed for night-time prayers. As best they could, they explained God to you. When you were of age, they insisted that you go to Confirmation classes. Through parents, God brings children to faith. As for myself, I can testify that if it were not for my mother's walking three miles each Sunday to church and Sunday school, I most probably would not be standing in this pulpit today. If it were not for the prayers of our parents in our behalf, we might never have been brought into the church or stayed in it.

You can cooperate with God in bringing people to conversion by simply witnessing in your own way. Through the years as a pastor I know of people who came to Christ and joined the church because some laymen took the time to make calls upon unchurched people in the community. A man once came to Spurgeon and said he was saved and wanted to bring others to Christ. He wanted to know how to do it. Spurgeon asked him, "What is your work?" The man replied, "I am a railroad engineer." Spurgeon inquired, "Is your fireman a Christian?" He answered, "I don't know." "Well," said Spurgeon, "Find out if he is not and start on him!" Is there anyone in your family not in church? God would use you to bring that person this Sunday. Is your neighbor going to church? If not, start working with him.

God can use your very life as a means of bringing people to conversion. There is a way to win other than making a call or saying something. It is by your daily life. It is a silent type of witness. People, unknown to you, watch you from day to day. They see something in you they do not possess. It is your sweet attitude. They see in you a quality of life they covet for themselves. They notice how you are unselfish, always putting others first. Your kindness and unselfishness speak to them in Christ. They want to be like you. Some day they may ask you what makes you tick, what is the secret of your radiance. Your good example will bring them to Christ.

Why should we be partners with God in bringing people to Christ? A low motive is fear. A minister once said to a convert, "I'm glad you saw the light." The convert replied, "I didn't. I felt the heat!" Why bring people to Christ? To build up the church? To gain self-satisfaction? To earn some merit with God? These are unworthy motives. A Christian wants to convert others because of his own experience with Christ. This relationship with Christ is so wonderful that he cannot help but share it with others. The knowledge of Christ is too good to keep. As a Christian you and I have strength through faith. We experience the peace of forgiveness. In Christ we have found the purpose of life and the reason for living. In it all is a marvelous joy. To work with God in bringing others that they, too, might have the same peace and joy.

How can you and I put others on fire for Christ if we ourselves are not burning? How can we sell a product if we ourselves have not bought the product? How can we convert the world if we as a church are not converted? This is the issue Christ in our Gospel lesson brings to our attention. Before he sent out the Disciples, the Gospel for today says "He called to him his twelve disciples. . ." Later it says, "These twelve Jesus sent out . . ." Before we go, we must come to Christ. Only then can we go to the world with the good news. The church must first gather before it can scatter into the world to witness and win. Before you go into the world today, come to Christ now!

What Do You Think You're Worth?
Pentecost V

"Are not two sparrows sold for a penny? And not one of them will fall to the ground without your Father's will. But even the hairs of your head are all numbered." (Matthew 10:29,30)

What do you think you're worth? It is not likely you are worth the billions of a Paul Getty or a Howard Hughes. Do you go to the other extreme when you would sell yourself for a nickel and give three cents change? Are you like the young lad who wore a football t-shirt with the letters 00, a double cipher? Was this the way he was telling the world that he felt he was less than nothing? It is not only what you think you are worth but what others think you are worth. What are you worth to your club, to your friends, to your employer, to God? One day a woman ran out of the house with the trash when she heard the garbage truck. She wore a ragged, bathrobe, worn-out slippers, her hair in curlers, and her face was coated with greasy cream. "Am I too late for the garbage?" she asked. "No, hop right in," came the reply. Maybe you think of yourself as garbage. An alcoholic once said to a preacher, "Tell me that I'm not a bum. Tell me I'm not junk."

In today's Gospel lesson Jesus gives the answer to our worth. It is not what you think of yourself, it is not what others think of your worth, but it is what God thinks you are worth. Jesus is teaching that it is better to fear God who can kill both body and soul rather than to fear man who can kill only the body. The reason you can trust God above man is because God has a higher evaluation of each person's worth. He refers to the minimal cost of two sparrows: two for a penny! He tells how God knows when one of these almost worthless creatures falls to the ground. God's knowledge of us is so detailed that he even knows the number of hairs on our heads.

Worth Everything

What do you think you are worth? The worldly man thinks he is everything. He is top value and there is nothing more important than he is. If he is not that, he wants to be. He will dream about it and strive to become somebody in the world. This was expressed by Archie Bunker, in "All in the Family." One day he said, "O Edith, I want to be on the team so bad I can taste it. And another thing. You should see the bowling shirts them Cannonballers got. All yellow silk, with bright red piping on the collar and sleeves." Edith replied, "And you look so good in yellow." Archie continues, "Yeah, I look good in yellow. And on the back there's a picture of a cannon firing a bowling ball at a set of pins. Beautiful. When you got something like that on your back, Edith, you know you're somebody."

The 1970s have been described as the "Me decade." Narcissism has been reborn in our time. You remember the Greek legend about Narcissus who saw his reflection in a pool and liked himself so well that he fell in love with himself. This is the generation that is preoccupied with self. We dwell on self-admiration, self-love, and self-concern. The "I" is the number one in our lives. In recent years we keep talking about and searching for self-identity, self-understanding, and self-fulfillment.

This is the age of humanism. We keep talking about the dignity and value of a human being. We appeal to people to be human. The greatest thing in the world, they say, is to be a human being. It is the ultimate value in life. This leads to the position that we are good people. Man is naturally and inherently good. We as humans have rights and we deserve the best. Commercials are exploiting this feeling among the masses. One commercial tells about a hair spray which costs more, but the punch line says, "It costs more, but I am worth it!" Another product advertises, "Be good to yourself." A hamburger chain says, "Have it your way." Another crys out, "You deserve a break today." All this reflects our concern with ourselves and our own importance.

This results in an inflated evaluation of our own importance. We become little gods, and the self in the center of our existence makes the self none other than God. It results in making a person think that he cannot do wrong or fail. A seven-year-old boy invited his Dad to come out to the back yard and watch him hit the ball. He said, "Look at this Dad," and he pitched the ball into the air, swung, and missed. "Strike one," he yelled. He did it a second time, "Strike two!" He explained, "It takes only one to be a hitter." He threw the ball into the air a third time and again he missed. "Strike three — you're out!" he shouted. Just then mother called them for dinner. As they headed for the house, he said, "Well, Dad, I guess that proved it. I really am a terrific pitcher!"

With this self-applause we can get to think of ourselves more highly than we ought to think. A sixteen-year-old girl wrote to Ann Landers, "What troubles me is that I have no problems . . . I am a pretty, mature girl. My figure is great, my skin is like peaches and cream. I have all the dates I can handle. My grades are tops and I win everything I try for at school. Something has to be wrong with me because nobody's perfect. What could it be?" With great wisdom and insight Ann Landers told her that her fault was that she was flawless. Haven't you met a person who never does anything wrong? Never admits a mistake? Never says, "I am sorry"?

If we are so good, then we will not believe in or practice self-control. This is often illustrated in parents who think that their little ones should not be curbed lest they be inhibited. Parents sometimes think that their children are always right and can do no wrong. A grandmother once wrote to Ann Landers about the way her daughter allowed her children to express themselves and not to hold anything back. If they are angry and feel hostility and fury, they are told to go to a "scream room" and let it out. The grandmother said she was taught to control herself and she wonders whether she was brought up the wrong way. Lack of self-control implies that a person is nothing but good and should not be curbed lest damage be done to the psyche. Could this be a reason for today's preoccupation with violence? We allow ourselves to express our passion to the hurt of other people.

This view of one's self leads to a false self-sufficiency. Andre Gide advises, "Believe in your strength and your youth. Learn to repeat endlessly to yourself: It all depends on me." This leaves God out of the picture. You do not need God. You can take care of yourself. All you need do is discover your potential and there is no end to what you can accomplish. Who in his right mind can accept that trash?

All of these forms of self-exaltation mean that modern man is self-centered and proud. It points to the one basic sin of mankind — self-assertion or the desire for recognition. This was the first sin in the Garden of Eden and the sin still stands.

Worth Nothing

What do you think you are worth? If you ask a true Christian, he will tell you that he is worth nothing in himself. A genuine Christian is not concerned about finding, but losing his identity in Christ. He is not out to find but to lose himself.

In our time we are told repeatedly that we are to love ourselves as a condition of loving others. Have we forgotten to hate ourselves? Jesus said that we must hate ourselves as a condition of being a follower of his. "If anyone comes to me and does not hate . . . even his own life he cannot be my disciple." At another time, Jesus taught that a disciple must deny himself, take up his cross, and follow him — if he wanted to be a disciple. It is denying self, not affirming, exalting, confirming self but saying "no" to self. That doesn't sound very modern, does it?

The greatest Christians have all had a very low opinion of their own worth. Listen to St. Paul: "I do not account my life of any value." In our language he is saying he does not consider his worth to be a penny's worth! In a great prayer, St. Augustine said, "Let me hate myself and love thee." Luther taught that God created something out of nothing. For God to create something out of us we must first be nothing. When he teaches about God's creation and preservation of us day after day, he says that God does all of this "without any merit or worthiness in me." When he explains how Jesus redeemed us, he says "who redeemed me, a lost and condemned creature." The great preacher, Spurgeon, put it this way, "Be content to be nothing, for that is what you are." Our hymns express this traditional view of a Christian's importance: "Would he devote that sacred head for such a worm as I?"; "Nothing in my hand I bring, Naked come to thee for dress, Foul I to the fountain fly;" and "Just as I am without one plea."

How and why does a Christian come to this apparently low opinion of himself? He reaches this estimate of himself when he confronts the greatness and the holiness of God. Then he sees himself in contrast to God. In 1976 when the "Today" show was featuring South Dakota, the cameras showed the fertile fields of the state and Mt. Rushmore with the four great presidents carved in the side of the mountain. In summing up South Dakota's land and people, the announcer said, "The sky and land are so immense that the people know their place." When you confront the immensity of God's infinite greatness, you realize your smallness. When you see the purity of Christ, you see your own filth. When Isaiah saw the holy and majestic God, he moaned, "I am undone, for I am a man of unclean lips." When Peter realized how good and great Jesus was, he fell down on his knees before him and said, "Depart from me, Lord, for I am a sinful man." In the sight of God I am nothing, for I see all my sins, my imperfections, my unworthiness, my helplessness.

Is this good or bad? It is bad if you look at it in terms of self-contempt. It is bad if you despise yourself as adding up to a cipher. To have a Christian's sense of worthlessness does not mean you despise yourself to the point of having no self-respect or self-esteem. If this results, it is a misunderstanding of the Christian's view of himself as nothing. On the other hand, this view of being nothing before God leads to a good thing — the highest and most difficult virtue; humility. The Christian has no reason to be proud, for he is nothing and he has nothing that God has not given him. He has no right to claim anything. He has no right to expect God to answer his prayers and do his bidding. I have no right to expect anything good from God as though I deserved it. I have no right ever to get angry with God or complain about bad luck. As I appear before God, I am inwardly urged to confess my sins and confess my unworthiness to be in his presence or to be his child. If there is any good in me, if there is any talent I possess, it is all from God. He gets the credit for any good in me.

Another good thing about this position is that it leads to exaltation. Jesus taught repeatedly that he who humbles himself will be exalted. God resists the proud but gives grace to the humble. The prophet, Samuel, said to King Saul, "When you thought little of yourself, God made you king." When Jesus humbled himself to be born of a virgin, to take the form of a servant, and to die on a cross, God highly exalted him and gave him a name above every other name. This happens to every Christian who approaches God in humility and a sense of nothingness. God lifts him from his knees and stands him on his feet and crowns him with life.

Worth Something

What do you think you're worth to God? As a secular person, you are led to think you are everything, the greatest good, the ultimate goal in life. Then you live for yourself and claim your rights as a human being. As a Christian, you stand before God and you see that you are nothing except what God can make out of you. But, what does God think about you and me? Are we of any value as persons to him or are we too small to be important to him? In our text Jesus points to God's high evaluation of the individual. He calls attention to the smallest items of creation and God's estimate of their value. Then he asks whether a human being is not worth as much as these.

God thinks you are something. You are valuable, you are important. This is based on the fact that God knows you personally and individually. Your importance is proved when a great person indicates that he knows you and can call you by name. Suppose you lived in "the sticks" and you came to the capitol city for a visit. The governor or the president met you on the street and indicated that he knew you. Would you be surprised? Honored? Would you be convinced that to the chief of state you were that important as to be known? In our text Jesus tells us — and who else would know better than he? — that God, the infinite, almighty Father in heaven, knows you not only by name but to the smallest detail of your being. Jesus says that God knows us so intimately that he knows how many hairs are on our heads. It has been computed that a blonde has 145,000 hairs, a brunette 120,000 hairs, and a red-head 90,000. This is on the average, but God goes one better than that. He knows how many hairs are on your individual head!

This means you are not too small for God's knowledge and concern. You are his creation and he knows what he made. And what he made, according to Genesis, was good. Even if nobody knows you or remembers you,

God does because you are that valuable to him. During the First World War the King of England sent a Christmas card to all the soldiers in the army. There was a soldier who had no friends or family. He was alone in the world. He received nothing for Christmas. Then the royal Christmas card came. He responded, "Even if no one else remembers me, my king does."

God considers you something also because God cares for you. The other morning we found a little bird lying helplessly on our patio. Perhaps it flew into the glass doors thinking it was open space and hurt itself. It could not fly and could use only one leg. I went out and picked up the bird and it fit into the palm of my hand. As I did, I thought of the words of our text that not a sparrow falls to the ground without God's will, consent, or permission. Could it be possible that God knew of this one little bird's falling? It is so great that it almost blows your mind. That bird is so important, so valuable to God that he knows and cares what happens to it.

Jesus taught from this that God is even more concerned with a human being than with a single bird of almost no value. This means God thinks a person is worth enough to be loved and cared for. Let us be sure we understand, though, that God does not love people because we have inherent worth or goodness. That is not the teaching of the Bible. Rather, man gets his value because God loves him in spite of his unworthiness to be loved. From the beginning man disobeyed God's laws and will. He has been a rebel and fought against God. He despised God and turned to gods who were no gods at all. Man has clothed himself with filthy rags, and he, like the Prodigal, went to a far country of sin to live it up and waste God's resources. It is similar to a child who lost his teddy bear. It originally cost only $10, but a reward of $100 was offered for its return. What made this teddy bear so valuable to the child? By now the teddy bear was old, worn, and ragged. It was the child's love for the teddy bear that made it so valuable and important to him. Man, too, can be worn-out and ragged and almost worthless in man's sight, but God considers him, as poor and worthless as he is, to be of inestimable value because he loves him. Paul expressed it beautifully, "Herein perceive we the love of God in that while we were yet sinners Christ died for us."

If we really want to see what value God places on us as individuals, we need just look at the cross. See those thorns — you were worth the pain! See those nails in hands and feet — you were the reason for it! See the agony of a miserable death — he died just for you! And don't forget who was on that cross. It was God's Son — "God was in Christ reconciling the world to himself." God so loved you that he gave his only Son. So that is what you mean to God. You are worth God's self-giving in Christ. It is almost too good to believe!

Since God thinks so much of me, then I as a person can have a sense of importance and value. I am not garbage nor junk. I am a child of God who makes me what I am. A person cannot understand who he is until he knows whose he is. All of our modern search for self-identity, self-understanding, and self-fulfillment leads to confusion and frustration because we cannot know nor find ourselves apart from God. Before joining the church, Jane Addams described her condition: "Weary of myself and sick of asking what I am and what I ought to do." She accepted Christ and joined the church. There she found the answer to who she was and what she ought to do. If you are troubled with the same problem in understanding your worth, turn to God and accept the truth in Christ. In a God-denying world the best thing we can do with self is to make a self-denying surrender to Christ.

The Cross Way of Life
Pentecost VI

"He who loves father or mother more than me is not worthy of me . . .and he who does not take his cross and follow me is not worthy of me. He who finds his life will lose it, and he who loses his life for my sake will find it." (Matthew 10:37-39)

During the presidential campaign of 1976, Jimmy Carter became famous for his teeth. Cartoonists had a holiday exaggerating the size of his teeth. His teeth were prominent because he went across the country constantly smiling which certainly was an important factor in his winning the presidency. Does life always let us smile? Are Christians supposed to wear a constant smile? Are there not times when a frown is more appropriate, times when we should be upset, angry, and ready to fight?

In today's Gospel lesson we see a side of Jesus seldom shown. The Prince of Peace is a disturber of the peace. He comes holding not an olive branch, the symbol of peace, but a sword which means fighting. Wherever Jesus goes, he stirs up controversy. He turns values upside down. He challenges sinful ways. He pits members of a family one against the other as they face the challenge of discipleship. How do you account for this? It is the result of Jesus' taking the cross road of life. If we follow him on this road, we can expect the same. This leads us to the cost of discipleship. Can we afford to be a true Christian? Do we want to pay the price of walking on the cross road of life? In our text Jesus calls us to follow him on this cross road. What is this road and what does it take to travel on this road through life?

The Road of Discipline

The cross road of life is the road of discipline. In our text Jesus says, "He who loves father or mother more than me is not worthy of me. . ." It is a call for self-discipline by putting Christ first in our way of life and all other persons in a subordinate relationship.

This matter of discipline is not a popular subject in affluent and luxury-loving America. As a seminary student in Philadelphia I often went downtown to famous Leary's bookstore located for many years next to the big department store, Gimbels. Repeatedly Gimbels approached Leary's store about purchasing the property in order to enlarge their store. Each time Leary's declined to sell. Finally a representative of Gimbel's said, "Just think of the price we are offering. With that you could be on Easy Street." Leary's store replied, "We don't want to be on Easy Street, we want to be on 9th Street." This is rare because most of us would rather live on Easy Street.

Our present society is characterized by the lack of discipline because we want to live on Easy Street. Many parents fail to discipline their children, resulting in spoiled brats. The daughter of a psychologist with a Ph.D. was put to bed with a sore throat. For the third time she was put to bed and finally her father at great length explained all the reasons why she should remain in bed. Finally she said, "Oh, Daddy, why don't you just *make* me?" Even children seem to know the value of discipline more than parents. It is claimed that discipline in our public schools is at its lowest ebb in the history of the school system. Competition is frowned upon because it is supposed to be damaging the child by creating pressure. Grades are bad because they are hard on the child's ego. The result is mediocrity and Johnny can't read. In 1976 the state of Florida passed a law that all graduating from high school had to be able to read and write! In addition, discipline is lacking in the commercial world. In 1975 an airplane crash that took seventy-two lives at the Charlotte, N.C., airport was, according to the post-crash investigation, due to lack of discipline in the cockpit. Instead of following prescribed procedures, the crew was busy discussing politics and used cars.

A Christian is one who practices the discipline of putting priorities in their proper order. It is the discipline of keeping your eye on the ball whether it is golf, tennis, basketball, or football. In our text Jesus is asking us to make him our first love. Then he goes on to discuss the love of members of a family whom we usually love more than any other person. Jesus is giving us a hard saying when he says that he must come first in our love and our family second. Anita Bryant, whose annual income from commercials and concerts is $500,000, once told a correspondent, "My priorities are God, husband, children, and country. I would die for all of them." This is the kind of relationship that Jesus would approve as one who was walking with him on the cross road of life. The cross means discipline by putting lesser loves in their place.

This matter of putting Christ above family is a common matter of discipline. Preachers like Sangster, Peter Marshall, and John Bunyan faced it and still face it. When Bunyan was put in jail for his preaching, he worried about leaving his family to fare for themselves, particularly his blind son. He wrote, "O the thought of the hardship I thought my blind one might go under, would break up my heart to pieces . . . But yet, recalling myself, thought I, I must venture you all with God, though it goeth to the quick to leave you; O I saw in this condition, I was a man who was pulling down his house upon the head of his wife and children; yet thought I, I must do it, I must do it."

It can happen to any layman, also. A young lady who had grown into Christian maturity became engaged in serious and meaningful prayer. She daily sought the will of God for her life. This led to resistance at home. Her parents called her a fanatic. They thought it was all right for her to go to church, but anything beyond that was going too far. By word and example her parents discouraged her in her Christian descipleship. When a member of a family puts Christ first in his life while the other members are disinterested, the conflict begins. The Christian wants to say grace before meals and the others laugh at him. The rest of the family is accustomed to using four letter words, but the Christian declines and they call him a "holy-holy." On Sundays the Christian gets up to go to church while the rest of the family sleeps late. Soon the Christian grows away from his family because he has higher values, and enjoys Christian friends. The discipline on the cross road of life is maintaining this first-love of Christ in the midst of a hostile environment.

A Road of Hardship

The cross road of life, in the second place, is a road of hardship. In our text Jesus says, "He who does not take up his cross . . ." The Christian way of life is the cross way. If it is a cross, why would it not be a road of hardship? The cross of Jesus is rough and tough. It means nails and a thrust of the spear. The cross calls for a sense of forsakenness and loneliness and agony and pain. The cross sheds drops of one's own blood.

But who wants to take that road of life? The other day I saw a bumper sticker which said, "Easy does it." That may be true in some cases but it is not the case when it comes to being and living as a Christian. The mood of people was expressed in a bank's full-page newspaper ad, "Paying without pain." It described a new way of paying bills — by telephone! In the Christian life, there is no paying without pain; there is the pain of a cross.

The American people are being called upon to voluntarily assume hardships because of the energy crisis. Some of the hardship is keeping your speed down to fifty-five, turning your thermostat during winter to 68 degrees, eating less that more food can be shared with the world's hungry, and refusing to waste natural resources by not littering with cans, paper, and bottles. Affluent Americans are beginning to realize that we cannot go on living without restraint as though there is always more where this comes from. We just cannot go on living as we have been, and the time has come to endure hardships. How many Americans are willing to practice these little inconveniences for the good of all? Not many because we have not taken up our cross. The time will probably come when the present voluntary hardships will become compulsory.

What hardships are we enduring as Christians? Compared with hardships of men like St. Paul — beatings, stonings, shipwrecks, cold, hunger, attacks by robbers — can we say that we suffer any hardships? Many of us are weak, soft, and flabby as Christians. It was announced at the Sunday morning service that the youth of the church would hold a "fastathon" for fifteen hours on Ash Wednesday. The youth offered to fast for adults at a certain hourly rate. The adults were asked to choose a youth they wanted to fast for them. The proceeds would go to the Hunger Appeal. It was a popular project because many would rather pay others to fast for them than to fast themselves. Also, take the matter of tithing. Is it not too hard for the majority? Getting up on a Sunday to go to church for worship is apparently too hard for sixty percent of the membership.

If we do not participate in the hardships of the cross, we are the losers. It is as the Romans said, *per aspera ad astra,* — through difficulties to the stars. We grow under the challenge of the difficult. President Harry Truman used to have a sign on his desk, "Bring me only bad news. Good news weakens me." When a famous artist first heard Jenny Lind sing, he said that if she would suffer for a year, she would sing like an angel. Later she did suffer for more than a year and it was said then she sang like an angel beside a sea of glass afire. Through suffering, pain, and hardship we become better persons. With this apparently in mind, Unamuno said, "May God deny you peace, but give you glory." Going with Jesus on the cross road involves hardship, and beyond the cross there is the glory of a crown of life eternal.

The Road of Sacrifice

The cross road of life, in the third place, is the road of sacrifice. This is brought out by Jesus in the text when he said, "He who loses his life for my sake will find it." Although it does not have four letters, the word, "sacrifice," is another dirty word along with hardship. The difference between the two words is that "sacrifice" is a dirtier word than "hardship."

John Morley, English statesman and writer, said in an address at Edinburg in 1887, "The great business of life is to be, to do, to do without, and to depart." Of the four central functions of life, "to do without" is the one most difficult, the one most of us never learn to acquire. Many of us are like the boy who said during the Second World War, "I wouldn't mind going to war and being a hero if I knew I wouldn't get hurt." The same reaction was expressed under church circumstances. A boy witnessed the high regard everyone had for a returned missionary; the crowds came to hear him. When his mother asked him what he wanted to be when he grew up, he replied, "I want to be a returned missionary!" So many of us would be willing to be a returned missionary, for we want to bless, not to bleed, to be good disciples but not to take discipline.

How much does the average person really sacrifice for the good of others or for Christ? For some it may be a sacrifice to tithe one's income. It may be like the bumper sticker that said, "If you love Jesus, tithe. Anyone can honk!" Probably only one percent of a church's membership tithes. That is not much sacrifice on the part of many. There are special times when a total sacrifice is made. Men make the sacrifice on the battlefield. A father lost his life while trying to rescue his son who had fallen through thin ice on a lake. A sheriff goes through a Colorado canyon to warn families of an oncoming flood and before he finishes, the flood washes him to death.

Sacrifices like these are unusual and exceptional. In our text Jesus is talking about every follower of his making a sacrifice by losing his life for Christ's sake. This kind of sacrifice is not a once-in-a-lifetime experience but a daily experience. It is not a sacrifice of death but a living sacrifice that goes on from day to day. It means a daily outpouring of one's self in the cause of Christ. It calls for giving, investing, expending, and throwing away one's life for Christ. It is pouring out your life in service to Christ and his people. This does not mean some special act of heroism but the general attitude and lifestyle of a person who daily forgets self and expends himself lavishly for the good of the Kingdom. It involves the daily giving of time and ability for others and for any good cause.

Whatever we do for Christ, can it be called a sacrifice? One time people referred to the sacrifice David Livingstone made by serving in Africa as a missionary. He remonstrated, "Can that be called sacrifice which is simply paid back as a small part of a great debt owing to our God, which we can never repay? ... It is emphatically no sacrifice. Say rather it is a privilege ... I have never made a sacrifice. Of this we ought not to talk, when we remember the great sacrifice which he made who left his Father's throne on high to give himself for us ..."

One thing about which we can be sure. There is no progress without an accompanying sacrifice. No business is built without the owner's sacrifice of hard work. No cause is won without someone's giving his all to it. No church is built without someone's laying down his life in service. This is even true with Jesus and our salvation.

The Bible says that without the shedding of blood, there is no redemption. To gain a crown, there must be a cross. What cause is worth your sacrifice? There is no virtue in just laying down your life for a cause, because it could be an unworthy cause. In our text Jesus specified the one and only worthy cause for the sacrifice of your life: "He who loses his life for my sake . . ." There it is, "for my sake."

The Road to Adventure

"Follow me" gives us the clue to the fourth road down which we must travel if we take the cross road of life. It is the road of adventure. The Jesus road is one of adventure because in following him you never know what is coming or what is going to happen to you. There is an unknown future. You have to take risks. There are real dangers ahead. This is what makes life with Christ exciting. Because you believe in him and want to be with him, you follow him regardless of what may come. When you walk after him as he leads, you give up your home security and your job security. You are out with him to right wrongs and to establish justice and a good life for society.

Why do this? It is the call of adventure. You cannot be content to sit down and slumber with the status quo. In 1 Kings there is a story about Hadad of Edom. When he was a child he had to flee to Egypt because David and his army came into Edom and killed every male person. In Egypt Pharoah gave Hadad a house, an allowance of food, and even his wife's sister for a bride. When Hadad learned that David died, he decided to return to Edom, but Pharoah asked, "What have you lacked with me that you are now seeking to go to your own country?" Hadad simply said, "Only let me go." Hadad could not be content to live in prosperity and security when his people needed him to break the yoke of Israel and get independence. It was an adventure of liberty.

When Jesus says to us, "Follow me," are we willing to follow him in every respect even though it means going to a cross? Many of us want to follow him in walking on water but not walking across the floor of a poor man's hovel. We, like Jesus, would follow by turning water into wine but we don't want to change money into food for the hungry. We would like to still the storm on the sea but not still the storm in a troubled heart. We don't mind following him when he walks on palm branches, but we do not want to walk after him in carrying the weight of the cross. We want the scepter of a king but not the staff of a shepherd. We would follow him as a king but we don't care to take up a towel and wash the dirty feet of beggars as a servant of Christ.

When Jesus says "Follow me," he is not standing behind but before us, leading the way. He sets the example of discipline, hardship, and sacrifice. Jesus never asks us to do what he himself would not do. He goes ahead of us as a pioneer, as a true leader. It is said that Teddy Roosevelt never said to his Rough Riders, "Go!" He said, "Come on, boys!" It is the case with every truly great leader of men. Each marched in the vanguard and challenged men to follow in their path. When Alexander the Great was in pursuit of Darius, king of Persia, he made his troops march 412 miles in eleven days. The men were about to die of thirst and could hardly go on. Some Macedonians with mules carrying skins of water came by and noticed how thirsty Alexander was. They filled a helmet with water and took it to him. Alexander looked around on his troops and saw how they longed for a drink. Then he returned the water saying, "If I alone should drink, the rest would be out of heart." The men became excited and charged ahead. In like manner, Jesus does not only go with us on this adventure, but he goes before us to show us the way and calling the very best from us. We are on an adventure to the promised land of life, liberty, and peace with god.

This is the cross-road of life, the road Christ took, the road Christians are called to take. But why should we, when people all around us are living on Easy Street? The people with whom we live take their leisure and love their luxury. Why take this hard road of the cross? At the end of today's Gospel lesson Jesus says a disciple of his will not lose his reward. Could that be the reason for going on this cross road? If there is a reward, the only one we would be interested in is the one expressed by Wilhelm Loehe when he said, "And what is my reward? I serve neither for reward nor thanks, but out of gratitude and love; my reward is that I am permitted to serve." I'll buy that as a reward. Will you?

Invitation to a New Life-Style
Pentecost VII

"Come to me, all who labor and are heavy-laden, and I will give you rest. Take my yoke upon you, and learn from me; for I am gentle and lowly in heart, and you will find rest for your souls. For my yoke is easy and my burden is light." [Matthew 11:28-30]

In his book, *The Greening of America*, Charles Reich claims that we are living during a transition from one age to another, from Consciousness II to Consciousness III, from the quantity of life to the quality of life, from things to values, from machines to men. This change constitutes a new revolution which will be an inner, non-violent type dealing with culture. To bring this about he says, "At the heart of everything is what we shall call a change of consciousness. This means a new head — a new way of living — a new man." The book is one of the most helpful and hopeful books produced in recent years and it signals promise for tomorrow's world. However, the one big failing of the book is that it fails to tell us how this new head, new heart, and new man are to be secured. The description of our present situation is very well done, but what good is it if we do not know how to bring about the solution? Reich does not have the answer, but Jesus does. We find it in our text. Jesus invites us to a new, better way of life or a new life-style. He says that if we will come to him, we will have this inner change that will result in a new life-style.

A New Goal

What is involved in this life-style which results from coming to Jesus? For one thing, it means we shall have a new goal for life. Jesus in our text says, "Come to me, all

who labor and are heavy-laden, and I will give you rest."
This means that Jesus should be the goal of our
existence. We are to come to him as the end of all things.
But, has he really been our goal during this generation?
If we are honest with ourselves, we will admit that not
God but gold has been our goal of life. We have been out
for money in terms of high wages and large profits. We
have said that what makes a man successful and what
gives him status is the amount of possessions he has in
terms of real estate, stocks, and bonds. There is no doubt
that materialism has been the passion of our lives.

We have to admit that we have been a tremendous
success at it, too. We boast that we are the richest nation
in the world, and we are proud of the fact that we have
the highest standard of living of any people of all time.
We have attained affluence. At least, give us credit for
that!

At the same time we must admit that we have been a
dismal failure at this business of making money. The law
of diminishing returns has begun to work on us. Our very
affluence is turning out to be our undoing. We have built
bigger and bigger machines to mass produce all kinds of
articles for our comfort and luxury. Now we have so
many things that we do not know what to do with the
discards and left-overs. Therefore, one of the biggest
headaches for us today is garbage disposal. For instance,
I took a portable phonograph to the shop to have it fixed.
The repairman said that it would cost as much to fix it as
a new one would cost. I decided not to get it repaired but
now I have it on my hands. No one will trade it in. No one
will buy it. What do I do with this thing? Where can I
discard it? Consequently, we see our whole landscape full
of discarded things.

Then we went into technology and industry to
manufacture the things for this affluent generation. To
produce these things we poisoned the air and polluted
the water. Ecologists tell us that at the present rate we
will smother ourselves in twenty years and we shall eat

ourselves into extinction. Moreover, we are proud of our mass production of autos, millions upon millions of them so that every family has at least two cars. Now we have reached the saturation point where we cannot find a parking space and when we get on the expressways there are so many cars that speed is cut to twenty miles per hour.

The result is that we are rich materially but poor spiritually. As the Psalmist said, "He answered their requests and gave leanness to their souls." This leanness of spirit is shown by our lack of rest which Jesus mentions several times in our text. We are so restless that one out of every five Americans moves each year. Each year we spend eighty million dollars on sleeping pills because we are so restless at night that we need help to get some sleep.

The time has come for us to realize that Jesus was right when he said that life does not consist in the abundance of things possessed. He also asked, "What shall it profit a man if he gain the whole world and lose his own soul?" In this coming new age, the goal of life needs to be Christ who came to bring us life, the quality of life. He said, "I am come that they might have life and that they might have it more abundantly . . ." To get this quality of life, we are to come to Jesus as the goal of our lives. Here in this text we are invited to come to Jesus by going forward to Jesus into a new life here and now. What we are learning is that this former life of things, machines, and materials just does not satisfy. There is more to life than these. We want peace, love, and freedom.

The new life-style is one that emphasizes and seeks the quality of life. To know the meaning of life and to get something from life, it would be better to drive a Mark IV Toyota than a Mark IV Continental. To have love, peace, and understanding in the family would be worth living in a $25,000 rather than a $50,000 house. In our time we find that there is no money for schools, libraries, music, and the arts but we have no difficulty raising money in terms of millions for apartment complexes and perimeter malls. If we had the quality of life as a goal, we would be glad to have less of the material things of life for those things that truly enrich life. But just try to sell this to labor unions and big corporations who demand ever higher wages and profits!

A New Mind

Coming to Jesus would result in a new man with a new heart and mind resulting in a new life-style. A second aspect of this style is a new mind for life. In our text Jesus brings this out when he says, "Take my yoke upon you and learn from me; for I am gentle and lowly in heart." This calls for a new mind, the mind of Christ. The mind is important for as a man thinks, so is he. Before we can do anything, we must think it through and get our thinking straight.

It is needless to remind you that much attention has been paid to the mind in recent years. We are in the midst of a knowledge explosion, and we so believe in getting an education that we say that unless you have a college education you cannot get a worthwhile job. But, what kind of knowledge do we have in this generation? One thing is for sure, we have carnal knowledge. Some of the best-selling books in recent months have titles like these: "All the Things You Wanted to Know About Sex and Were Afraid to Ask," "The Sensuous Woman," and "The Sensuous Man." This is the generation that knows all about sex down to the smallest physical detail. We know more about the physical side of procreation and seem to enjoy it the least of any people in history. And, of course, we have scientific knowledge that is truly amazing. It may be the implantation of an artificial heart or the placing of a man on the moon. It is something for man to place men on the moon within a few hundred feet of their destination after projecting the capsule over

250,000 miles. Our technical and scientific know-how is truly fantastic and you cannot help falling down in awe at the mind of man.

All well and good, but how do we stack up in spiritual knowledge? Here is where we are like the people in the time of the prophets who said that there was a famine in the land for the word of God. It is tragically true that our spiritual knowledge is almost nil. We are religiously morons. We are illiterate in biblical knowledge. We have been so very busy making money that we have not been able to obey the Psalmist, "Be still and know that I am God."

Jesus invites us to have a new mind for the new age. He says, "Learn from me." What can we learn from Jesus about God and ourselves? We can learn who we are. And when we know who we are, we gain humility. Jesus says, in our text that he is gentle and lowly in heart. In Philippians Paul beautifully describes Jesus' humility by saying that we should have this mind which was also in Jesus who did not think it robbery to be equal with God, but emptied himself, took the form of a servant, and became obedient unto death, even the death of the cross. How do you get this kind of a mind? It comes as a byproduct of putting God first in your life. If you have a God-centered life, you will live to serve, please, and glorify God. You will see God in everything that happens. The slogan of your life will be "How good of God!" How good of God to give to you life, to bless you with strength, to lead you daily into paths of service, to allow you to accomplish some good. When God is the source of your strength, you do not take any credit for anything you might accomplish. God rightfully deserves all the praise. This makes you humble, because God is first and you are second.

This leads to a humility of service. One of the most impressive scenes in Jesus' life is when he takes a basin and towel and washes the feet of his disciples. One Maundy Thursday this was enacted in our Seminary chapel when the Dean washed the feet of several students and faculty. It was an unforgettable experience to see the head of the school kneeling down before his "underlings" and doing this humble service. This answers the question, "What shall I do with my life?" We are here to serve, and Jesus said that he who would be first shall be servant. Life is for giving and not for getting. Jesus taught that he who loses his life for his sake would find it. It is not a matter of asking what God can do for you but what you can do for God. The investing, throwing away, and abandoning the self in the larger field of service of God and man results in humble service. This is the style of life for the new age. Only coming to Jesus can make a man humble. This we learn from Jesus.

A New Dynamic

The Christian life-style, in the third place, involves a new dynamic for life. In our text Jesus says, "My yoke is easy and my burden is light." It is easy and light because of a dynamic that makes it this way.

How many of us think that it is easy to live the Christian life in a godless world? We love to say how hard we must fight against temptation. We tell of our struggle against disappointments and frustrations. We seem to like to tell how hard it is to be a Christian because we love the martyr role. If the Christian faith and life is hard for us, it is because we are living on the level of the law rather than on the high plane of grace. We think of life in terms of rules, regulations, obligations, and responsibilities. We talk in terms of "must" and "ought." Indeed, this kind of living is tough and rough. But this is not the Christian style of life.

Jesus' way of life is easy because it is motivated by love. It is not hard to love, is it? You love because you love. What you do for others is done gladly and willingly. When you love, your primary purpose is to please him.

Nothing is considered a higher honor than being able to do something to help that person. It is not a chore or a duty, but a joy. One time David Livingstone was praised for his great sacrifice in going as a missionary to Africa. He replied that for him it was not a sacrifice at all but it was a high privilege to go and tell the gospel. Love is the key to making a burden light and a yoke easy. How do we get to love that this might be so? We love people because we love God. We love God because he first loved us in Christ. And the more we love God, the more we will love our fellowman and in this love we will find ease and pleasure. To do his will is not hard because we love to please God. To obey his commands is easy because his will is our will. The cross he lays on our shoulders is not heavy but is as light as a feather because we take it up in love for him.

It is easy to be a Christian, moreover, because we possess the Spirit of God. The Spirit gives us the willingness and the power to do the things we should do. Out of the Spirit come various virtues as Paul lists them in Galatians: joy, love, peace, patience, self-control, etc. These are called fruits of the Spirit. To talk about fruit, reminds us of fruit trees. Did you ever see a tree groan under the load of having to bear fruit? Have you ever noticed a tree sweating because of the hard work to produce an apple? Did you ever see a tree that was writhing in pain over having to produce an abundance of fruit? That is silly, isn't it? We know that a tree silently, gladly, normally and naturally produces fruit because it is its business and mission in life to bear fruit. The same can be said about a Christian and the fruits of the Spirit. If the tree is a good one, good fruit will result. If one possesses the good spirit, good works will result. The virtues will be produced as fruit just as spontaneously, normally, and naturally as breathing. That is our mission when we are in the Spirit. If this is so, then it behooves us to get the Spirit of God in our lives. For this we should pray daily and use those means by which the Spirit may come to us. A true Christian does not try to be a Christian. He does not work at it. He does not say that he must now shape up and be a better person. That is drudgery and misery. That is hard. The easy way is Christ's way of the Spirit who gives us power to be and do all that is expected of us as Christians.

In our sober and serious moments every one of us will admit that we feel that need of being a better person and living a better life. We also will agree that we need a more Christian order of society. How shall we get it? We have tried many things and the cures have been worse than the disease. It is like a pill that is supposed to give a bald man hair overnight. The trouble is that it causes him a heart ailment. To overcome the heart trouble, he is given another pill which causes defective vision. To remedy the vision problem, another pill is given but it causes a man to lose his hair. So, he is right back where he started from. He is no better off, if not worse off. In recent years we have been trying all kinds of things to improve ourselves and the world, but are we any better off? There is one way to bring in this new age about which Reich writes. The solution is Jesus. Indeed, we unashamedly confess that Jesus is really the answer and the only answer to a better world and a finer person. So, Jesus now stands before us with open arms and with love and tenderness in his eyes and voice. He invites us to a new style of life when he says, "Come to me." If we do, we shall have that new life-style which will fit us for the new age to come.

It Takes Two to Preach!
Pentecost VIII

That same day Jesus went out of the house and sat beside the sea. And great crowds gathered about him, so that he got into a boat and sat there; and the whole crowd stood on the beach. And he told them many things in parables, saying: "A sower went out to sow. And as he sowed, some seeds fell along the path, and the birds came and devoured them. Other seeds fell on rocky ground, where they had not much soil, and immediately they sprang up, since they had no depth of soil, but when the sun rose they were scorched; and since they had no root they withered away. Other seeds fell upon thorns, and the thorns grew up and choked them. Other seeds fell on good soil and brough forth grain, some a hundredfold, some sixty, some thirty. He who has ears, let him hear." [Matthew 13:1-9]

It takes two to tango, two to play tennis, two to fight, two to make love, and it even takes two to preach. Maybe you never thought of that because you probably considered preaching to be the pastor's sole function. Paul was half right when he asked, "How can they hear without a preacher?" The other half is, "How can they preach without a hearer?" We need to understand that preaching is a two-way street, not a monologue but a dialogue between pulpit and pew. If there is a broadcaster, there must be a receiver; if a speaker, then a listener. It is like the speaker who began his message by saying, "Both of us have a task to perform: I am to speak and you are to listen. I hope you will not get finished before I do!"

Communicating the Word of God depends as much upon the listener as upon the preacher. If the hearer shuts his mind, the speaker may as well hush. If the hearer gets only a part of the message, to that extent the speech was a failure. Jesus faced this problem one day when he preached to a crowd along the Sea of Galilee. Our Gospel lesson for today paints the picture of Jesus sitting on the beach and soon crowds come to hear him preach. To avoid getting pushed into the water, he borrows a boat, sits down, and begins to preach by telling the parable of the sower. The seed falls on four different kinds of ground, but only one produces results. Later he explains that this is the way it is with people who hear the Word of God. He pleads for better listening as he cries, "He who has ears, let him hear."

To Preach Is To Hear

If it takes two to preach, then the laity can preach, too! Pulpit and pew are partners in preaching. The one is as important as the other. This may seem foolish to you and you may be asking, "How can I in the pew take part in the preaching?" One way is to be a hearer, to be present to hear the sermon. There can be no preaching without hearers. Without hearers, the preacher is talking to deaf pews and is wasting his time and energy. It is like television. There can be a powerful and first-class station telecasting the most important news but if there is no TV set to receive the telecast, what good is the presentation of the program? Jesus, at the time of telling the parable of the sower, did not have this problem. Our text says, "Great crowds gathered to hear him." Can't you see the mass of people lined up on the beach? Can you see Jesus sitting in the boat rocked gently by the lapping waves on the shore? This was not the only time, for once he was preaching in a house so crowded that they had to let a paralytic down through the roof to be healed!

In a sense, the church in American has her crowd, too. On a given Sunday it is estimated that eighty-five million people are gathered in our churches while only five and one-half million assemble for sports events in a year. Should we be content with eighty-five million on a Sunday to hear the Word of God? This represents only forty percent of the church's members. In addition, forty percent of Americans have no church connection. If all our people would come to hear the Word, we would have an Easter attendance every Sunday. Isn't it a shame that more people do not come to hear the Word? From week to week pastors inviting people to worship hear lame, old excuses like the two men who were fishing on a Sunday morning. The one said to the other, "I couldn't have gone to church today anyway, because my wife is sick in bed." Excuses. excuses; "it is too hot, too cold; you are too tired, or too busy!" The tragedy is that those not present need so badly to hear the Word. Have you ever said after a sermon, "I wish the whole world could have heard that!"? Because the person was not present, the sermon was in vain. For that absentee, there was no sermon. Do you see how important you are in the function of preaching? Your presence for preaching is as necessary as the preacher's presence in the pulpit.

Why should we and all people come to church to hear the Word preached? It is because the preached word is God's Word. The sermon is not the minister's opinion or philosophy of life. As long as he is faithful to his text taken from the Bible, the Word of God, God is speaking through him to you, the people. One time while the sermon was in progress, a little boy whispered to his mother, "Is that God up there speaking?" If the man in the pulpit is true to the Word, it is truly God speaking. Can there be anything or anyone more important than God? Is God not more important to hear than the president of the USA, or the governor of a state, or a learned scholar, or a business tycoon? Luther explained the meaning of the command, "Remember the sabbath day . . ." by saying, "We should so fear and love God as not to despise his Word nor the preaching of the gospel, but deem it holy and willingly hear and learn it."

Why do we need to hear God's Word preached? We need to hear the commands of God. If we do not, how then can we obey his commands? When judgment day comes, we cannot plead that we did not know the commands of God. Ignorance is not excuse for disobedience. Do you hear God saying to you, "Repent or perish," "The wages of sin is death," and "Do this and you shall live"? Also, we need to hear God's gracious promises. There is good news coming from the pulpit directly from God's mouth. When we are troubled, when our burdens are too heavy, when we are plagued with guilt, God has some wonderful news for us: "He who comes to me I will in no wise cast out;" "If we confess our sins, God is faithful and just to forgive our sins;" "My grace is sufficient for you;" "Fear not, for I am with you. Be not dismayed, for I am your God . . ." Counting those inactive in our churches and those not members of a church, it is said that three out of every four American adults need to find and accept Christ as Lord and Savior. Where are they going to hear about Christ except they come to hear the Word? It simply gets down to this: no hearer, no preaching.

Preach by Receiving the Word

It does take two to preach. You, the hearer, are as important as the preacher. You take part in the preaching by just being present to hear the Word. Is that enough? You may have a TV set in your home, but what if you do not have it turned on? It is obvious that the TV set is no good unless it is turned on to receive the telecast. That is easy enough to understand, isn't it? The same applies to preaching. It is not enough for you to be physically present in church to hear the Word. You need to be turned on to receive the message. You know, don't you, that you can turn off the preacher and not hear a word he says? A preacher can be rejected and ignored. The Bible is full of instances of this very thing. Amos was told to go home and preach to his own country. Two kings listened to four hundred prophets rather than to the true prophet, Micaiah, because he told them the truth that hurt. When Jeremiah preached, the people laid hold of him and shouted, "You shall die!" When Jesus preached in his home town, the people threatened to throw him headlong over a cliff. At another time when Jesus finished his sermon, the people took up stones to throw at him. Now if Jesus could not get a hearing, how possible it is for people today to refuse to hear the Word!

The hearer to be a part of preaching must take the Word into his mind and heart. This is a problem of the soil that Jesus mentioned in the parable. Only one of the four kinds of soil received the seed. The other three kinds of soil did not take the seed or, if they did, the ground was too shallow or weeds choked the seed. Could this be the way it is in our congregation? Are only one-fourth of the worshipers taking the Word into their lives? When we see how little results from a sermon in terms of repentance, reformation, and service, the proportion probably still holds true.

How can you take the seed of the Word into the soil of your life? How can you get turned on with the gospel? For the Word to enter, the soil must be open. There needs to be open minds and hearts for the Word to come and abide. As you know, it is possible to have a closed mind and heart. You can sit in church and look up to the pulpit and say under your breath, "I dare you to change my mind." You can say, "Don't preach to me because I already have my mind made up about that subject." You can be smug and self-satisfied, and even feel that you know it all. There is a Flat Earth Society which believes that the earth is flat. Even when astronauts went to the moon and took pictures from outer space showing the earth as a globe, they still do not accept the fact that the earth is not flat. In contrast to that closed mind, you, as a hearer, need to be wide open desiring new knowledge, new insights, new life. To get that openness, prayer is a big help. Before coming to church or right before the sermon, pray that you might be receptive to God's Word in order for God to help you. It would help, too, if you would pray for the preacher. In a Mississippi congregation a letter went out to each member from the Commission on Membership asking the people to form a conspiracy by agreeing to pray for their pastor while he preaches. This will not only help him to be a better preacher but will help you to be open to the Word.

To receive the Word into your mind and heart, you need to concentrate on the message while it is delivered. We need to pay attention to what is being said. This calls for a discipline of the mind. It is said that out of every minute, the mind listens for ten seconds and wanders off the other fifty seconds. While sitting in the pew during the twenty-five or more minutes of the sermon, it is easy to think of other things; what you did last night, what you will prepare for Sunday dinner, what schedule you have this coming week, where you need to go tomorrow, the people you need to see, and so forth. These wandering thoughts must be brought into subjection. Keep your eye on the preacher and let him talk to you as though you were the only one present. Concentration also calls for shutting out distractions that may disturb your listening. There may be loud noises outside the church, latecomers, teen-agers whispering in the pew behind you, a crying child, a person getting up to go to a restroom, the antics of a choir member in full view of the congregation, a bee or a fly sailing around. The good listener will, as far as possible, ignore these distractions and will do all in his power to remove such distractions from the next service. His mind is set on the Word and he takes it all in. Only then is he preached to and only then does the act of preaching really take effect. The good soil is the receptive soil.

Preach by Understanding

The hearer may be present to hear the Word. He may go even further and listen to the Word. But, if he does not understand what he is hearing, the preaching does no good. The layman in the pew is a partner in preaching to the extent that he understands God's Word for his times and world. Think of it again in terms of a TV set. You can have one; you can turn it on. But, is it properly tuned? When we moved to our apartment, we saw, in the living room, an antenna wire which we attached to our TV set. But, the reception was far from satisfactory. The sound was cloudy and the picture was distorted. We were at the point of buying a new set. Before doing it, we called the rental office and asked about the TV antenna. We were told that this was not an outside antenna but a cable antenna which we could rent by the month. When we contracted for the cable service, our TV worked perfectly. Now we could understand what was being said and shown. In the parable some seed falls on good ground and brings forth fruit. What constitutes good soil? Jesus said the good soil is that which understands what is heard.

When you hear something, do you get it all? Do you get the real meaning? Do you get all the facts? How do you hear? What do you get out of it? A college president sent the following message to his vice-president: "Next Thursday at 10:30 a.m. Haley's Comet will appear over this area. This is an event which occurs only once every seventy-five years. Call the division chairmen and have them assemble their teachers and classes on the athletic field and explain this phenomenon to them. If it rains, then cancel the day's observation and have the classes meet in the chapel to see a film about the comet." This message went from the vice president to the division chairmen to the teachers to the students who in turn wrote home to their parents: "When it rains next Thursday at 10:30 over the college athletic field the phenomenal seventy-five year old president of the college will cancel all classes and appear before the whole school in the chapel accompanied by Bill Haley and the Comets." When the service is over and you go home, what do you report the preacher said to the one too sick to worship that day? Is the message distorted and garbled? Did he really say that? Many a preacher gets into trouble when people say he said things he did not say in his sermon.

How can you receive the Word with understanding? You need to have some knowledge to really understand what is preached. When Samuel was a boy, God called him but he thought it was Eli calling him. The Bible explains, "Now Samuel did not yet know the Lord, and the Word of the Lord had not yet been revealed to him." To understand the Word, we need to know the Bible, to know God, to know Christ, the cross, and our human condition. In addition, we need faith to understand. You need faith that the preacher's message is God's Word, faith to believe and accept the promises of God. Believers understand what God is saying to them in and through the Word. Where there is no faith, there is no acceptance of the Word. This was the problem in Nazareth. The people did not believe in Jesus, for they cynically asked, "Is this not Joseph's son?" The problem was faced by the author of Hebrews when he explained, "The message which they heard did not benefit them, because it did not meet with faith in the hearers."

Understanding of the Word depends, too, on the hearers' possession of the Spirit. The non-spiritually minded do not know what he is talking about when the preacher speaks of spiritual matters. It is like a grade school graduate going to a learned lecture on astrophysics. He is there and he is listening, but it is all "Greek" to him. He does not have the background to understand what is being said. When God's Word is proclaimed, for those without the Spirit, the Word is only man's opinions. He does not feel God's presence. Nor does he hear God's Word coming in a man's words. In

Shaw's play, *Saint Joan,* an archbishop asks Joan, "How do you know you are right?" Joan replies, "I always know. My voices . . ." King Charles interrupts, "Oh, your voices, your voices! Why don't the voices come to me? I am king, not you." Softly Joan responds, "They do come to you, but you do not hear them. When the Angelus rings, you cross yourself and have done with it; but if you prayed from your heart, and listened to the thrilling bells in the air after they stop ringing, you would hear the voices as well as I do." We do hear what we want to hear. If we have the Spirit, we will hear spiritual truth with understanding.

Preach by Responding

As a worshiper you, too, can preach, but do you? You do not if you are only present to hear, if you only take it in, even if you understand what is preached. Preaching is not complete until there is a response. Martin Buber once said, "He who ceases to make a response ceases to hear the Word." In the parable, Jesus emphasized that the good soil produced fruit in various measures: one hundred, sixty, and thirty-fold. He who hears and understands the Word is expected to obey the Word, to put it into practice. A part of hearing is listening in terms of obeying what is heard. A mother took her ten-year-old boy to a doctor to get his ears examined, because it seemed to her he had difficulty in hearing. When, after a lengthy examination, no physical cause was found, the doctor put his hand on the boy's shoulder, looked him in the eye, and asked, "Son, do you have any trouble hearing?" The little fellow quickly answered, "I don't have trouble hearing, Doctor. I just have trouble listening." When Jesus was transfigured, the voice of God said to the three Disciples, "This is my beloved Son with whom I am well pleased; listen to him." It was not only listening to Jesus' words but *obeying* the words of Jesus. How often a parent says to a child, "Now you listen to me!" and the child knows Mother means that she is to be obeyed!

How does one respond to a sermon? The hearer responds while the sermon is in progress. Preaching is communication, a dialogue. The listener may respond to the preacher verbally by saying, "Amen," "Preach on!" or "Hallelujah." If there were more of this, the preacher would be encouraged to be more bold and energetic. As a hearer, you communicate to the preacher non-verbally also. You say a lot to a preacher if your eyes are looking out the window, or looking at the preacher. Your restlessness in the pew sends a message to the pulpit. Looking at your watch during the sermon tells the preacher you are bored. Your attitude can support or detract from the spirit of the speaker. If you are with him, if you are encouraging him, if you are praying for him, this will be felt by the preacher and will encourage him. Behind every great preacher is a great listening congregation. The responding congregation helps the preacher to be his very best. The people seem to draw the Word out of him and he often preaches beyond himself as the people seem to say, "Tell us more, preacher. Give it to us, preacher!"

There should be an even greater response when the sermon is over. A sermon was meant not only to be heard and enjoyed but to be lived. The pastor delivers the sermon to the church on Sundays to be delivered to the world throughout the rest of the week. In church the people hear a sermon. During the week the world should see that sermon in the daily life and conversation of the people. A layman preaches that sermon at home, in the office, and at the club. A lady heard a sermon on the poverty of the third world, and the next day her pastor saw her taking a car load of old clothes for overseas shipment. There the sermon was in action. A man heard a sermon on the need to make the church more effective in the community by more active participation in the work of the church. That night the preacher received a call from him saying that the pastor should call on him for any service he felt he could do. One time St. Francis asked a few of his followers to go with him to the village to preach. They went from place to place, greeting people, lending a hand where necessary, and just being available and friendly. One of the brothers complained, "I thought we were to preach, but now we are back and no sermon was given." Francis patiently explained, "All the time we were talking and visiting with the people, we were preaching."

When we built our new church in Atlanta, I asked the architect to have inscribed on the front of the pulpit, in large letters for the whole congregation to see, these words from Jeremiah: "O earth, earth, earth, hear the word of the Lord." That is the cry of the church today: "hear the Word of God," really hear it. This is God's appeal, too: "Incline your ear, and come to me; hear, that your soul may live." "He who has ears, let him hear" what God has to say. But he with the ears will not hear unless herald and hearer say it together.

Holy Tares!
Pentecost IX

Another parable he put before them, saying, "The kingdom of heaven may be compared to a man who sowed good seed in his field; but while men were sleeping, his enemy came and sowed weeds among the wheat, and went away. So when the plants came up and bore grain, then the weeds appeared also. And the servants of the householder came and said, to him, 'Sir, did you not sow good seed in your field? How then has it weeds?' He said to them, 'An enemy has done this.' The servants said to him, 'Then do you want us to go and gather them?' But he said, 'No; lest in gathering the weeds you root up the wheat along with them. Let both grow together until the harvest; and at harvest time I will tell the reapers, Gather the weeds first and bind them in bundles to be burned, but gather the wheat into my barn.'" [Matthew 13:24-30]

One night David Brinkley closed the NBC news telecast by telling of a Swedish pastor who pronounced the Benediction after which a man stood up and addressed the pastor, "If you don't stop running after my wife, I'm going to thrash you." A pastor running after another man's wife? In St. Petersburg, Florida, self-appointed evangelist, John 3:16 Cook, was arrested twice in one month, once for drunken driving and the other time for strong-arm robbery. A drunken, stealing evangelist? Soon after the Episcopal church approved women for the ministry, a bishop ordained a lesbian. A minister a lesbian? A minister murders his wife and child in Florida. Can a Christian leader be a murderer?

Could it be that these are church members, and leaders at that? How can this be? Isn't the church the communion of saints, the body of Christ, the salt of the earth, and the light of the world? Are these rare exceptions or does the church consist of many such sinners? We should not be shocked that these things happen in the church, for Jesus taught in today's parable of the wheat and the weeds that we can expect weeds among God's wheat. The church is a combination of holy saints and holy tares!

Wheat and Weeds

The parable in our text tells us about the holy tares in the church. It reminds us, for one thing, that the church consists of wheat and weeds, good and bad, and saints and sinners. The church is not a museum of perfect saints but a school of sinners. While we are shocked with the sinful behavior of some church people, we must not forget that the field of the church consists primarily of wheat. In spite of special sinners, the church has the best people on earth. Compared to the world, members of the church are the kindest, most caring, and most highly principled of all people. Most members take their religion seriously and sincerely. They have Jesus as their model and they long to be like him in their daily lives.

On the other hand, we need to realize that there are weeds in God's field, the church. If we do not realize this fact, we will become disillusioned and disgusted with the church. Many of us may have a romantic and idealistic view of the church as a place where the people are as good as gold. When the truth is known, these often quit the church or if not members, they refuse to join it. Have you not heard someone say "I am not going to join a church because there are too many hypocrites in it"?

So, let's be honest and face up to the facts, lest you get an unrealistic picture of the people in the church. Are there hypocrites in every church? Indeed, there are. A minister, walking down a street, saw a crowd of boys with a dog in their midst. He walked over to them and asked them what they were doing. One said, "We are having a contest to see who can tell the biggest lie. The one who tells the biggest gets the dog as a prize." The minister was horrified and said, "That's terrible! You know it is wrong to tell a lie. Why, when I was a boy, I never told a lie!" One little fellow turned to the minister and said, "Here, mister, you win our puppy dog!"

Some people are in the church because of expediency, to see what they can get out of it for their own profit. Many are like a secretary to a librarian who was retiring and was given a farewell dinner. At the close of the librarian's farewell speech, the gathering gave her a standing ovation, all except her secretary. When the meeting was over, someone approached her and asked why she acted so disrespectfully. If she felt that way about her former boss, why did she come to the dinner? She explained, "Well, I heard it was going to be a good meal and I was hungry." Some belong to the church for the status the church gives. They want to belong to "First" Church in order to have a classy place for a future wedding or a dignified funeral. It may be that some want to profit economically by belonging to a church, like the funeral director joined one church, his wife another, and their daughter a third church, in order to get the funeral business from all three churches. For those running for office, it may be smart to belong and go to a church to become visible and to give a good impression. When the election is over, the candidate is not seen again until Christmas.

Yes, there are weeds in the church represented by those who are not consistent in their faith and life. One night a tenant stole a goose from the owner's poultry house. The next Sunday both owner and tenant were in the same church service. The tenant got happy and began to shout praises to God. After the service, the owner said to the tenant, "How could you have the gall to shout 'Praise the Lord' when you know full well that you stole my goose Friday night?" The tenant grinned and said, "Lordy mercy, Mister Jones! I ain't gonna let no old dead goose keep me from shoutin' about my Lord!"

Why does this situation exist in every church? God does not want it this way. It would bring tears to the eyes of Jesus. The church herself is unhappy about the condition. Why is this? That is the question raised by the servants in the parable, "How, then, has it weeds?" The owner explained, "An enemy has done this." The enemy of God, Satan, has sown bad seed into God's field. The Devil can and does enter the hearts of individual Christians and can enter and work in a church. Right after his famous confession, "Thou art the Christ," Peter became the spokesman of Satan when he tried to discourage Jesus from going to the cross. Jesus had to say to him, "Get behind me, Satan!" Some church members can have the devil in them and can work for him even inside the church. Once a white man bought a black church, but when the time came for the congregation to vacate the building, they delayed in doing so. The buyer tried to be patient and waited for a long time, but the congregation refused to move out. Finally, he planned a strategy to get them out. He had someone during a night service pull the main switch and the church was in total darkness. Then he had someone pull his car up at the back of the church with the lights on. The buyer, dressed in a devil's suit, came through the window and was silhouetted by the car lights as he started down the center aisle. The members scrambled for the exit as fast as they could, just scared to death that the devil would catch them. But one lady was in a wheelchair and she could not go very fast. When the devil came close to her, she held him off by saying, "Now listen here, Devil. I want to you to know that I have been in this church every time the doors were opened. I have been a Sunday School teacher for twenty-five years, and I have been president of the Women's Society for thirty years. And I want you to know, Satan, that I have been on your side all the time!"

It may be the church's own fault that there are many unworthy members in the church. It could be the result of the church's low membership standards. It is harder to join a club or a fraternity than it is to join a church. The church asks no questions about the personal life of prospective members. It makes no investigation of the character of the candidate. Unlike some clubs, a church member does not have to be voted in as a member. Instead, the church goes out to every Tom, Dick, and Harry and begs them to join, as though they would be doing the church a favor by joining. This has resulted in a condition that often smells to high heaven. It is as someone once said, "The church is like Noah's ark. If it were not for the storm outside, you could not stand the stench inside." This is not a pretty picture of the church, but you need to know it as it is lest you be disillusioned and disappointed. In the parable, Jesus taught that there are holy tares in the wheat.

"Throw Out the Bums!"

What are we to do with these people in the church who are not living up to the teachings and example of Christ? The first thing we human beings think of is, "Throw out the bums!" In the parable the servants ask the farmer-owner, "Then do you want us to go and gather them?" This seems to be the natural and sensible thing to do. If there is a rotten apple in the barrel, get rid of it as fast as you can to prevent the other apples from rotting. When a school board has convincing evidence that a teacher is a Communist, it is not long before that teacher's resignation is demanded. When a laborer is loafing on the job, he is given two weeks' notice before being fired. In a law office a secretary was required as part of her work to make coffee for the lawyers. She refused to do it and was let go, but she in turn sued the firm for sex discrimination. Because Wilbur Mills, chairman of the House Ways and Means Committee, was getting drunk and fooling around with Fanny Foxe, he was dropped from the Masonic Order. When it was learned that Wayne Hays had Elizabeth Ray on the Federal payroll as his mistress, he was forced to resign as a member of Congress. Even in the case of the presidency of the United States, a man who felt he was above the law of the land was compelled to go into retirement.

We think we have good reasons for getting the "bad eggs" out of the church. When people do not live up to the moral standards of the church, they bring shame and disgrace upon the good name of the church. The late Pierce Harris once told of a golfing friend who did a lot of good but did not belong to a church. Pierce tried to get him into a church, but he failed. After one try, the friend said, "I like you. I know you are sincere. I appreciate having you for my friend. But — I know too many people who belong to the church — some of them yours — who are not as good *in* the church as I am *out* of it. You want the picture I have in my mind of an average church member? Mix a little Christianity with a few cocktails and some silly conversation and you've got the picture of my idea of the average churchman." Pierce Harris then commented, "Some church members are not a blessing to the world. They have done this man more damage than the blackest sinner. They may have sent his soul to hell . . . .".

Unworthy church members should be dismissed because they reduce the good influence of the church upon the world. Insincere members weaken the witness of the church. It is reported that in a year, five and one-half million Americans go to an athletic event, but on an average Sunday, eighty-five million are in church. There is no other event or cause that can gather together that many people. Think for a moment what could happen for good in this country if eighty-five million people week after week lived their religion. Why doesn't the church have more impact upon American society? How can crime flourish as it does when there is a church on almost every corner? One reason for the lack of influence is the poor quality of church members. Nietzsche, an atheist, once wrote, "Redeemers you must show yourselves to be, if I would believe your Redeemer."

We think we ought to get rid of the pseudo-Christians in our churches because they are poisonous to the rest of the church. Some interpreters say that the weeds are darnel, a plant that looks like wheat until it matures and a plant whose seeds are poisonous. Insincere members spread the poison of their bad spirit through gossip or through a bad example to other members of the church. The poor example turns good Christians off the church. A devout lady was trying to get her boss to come back to church and renew his faith. In the same office was a man who professed to be a strong churchman to the extent of bringing his Bible daily to work with him. Yet he consistently sneaked away from work twenty to thirty minutes each day. After having reprimanded the man three times, the employer told the lady, "That's why I don't go to church! That fellow is supposed to be a Christian and he can spout the Bible verses for hours on end — yet he consistently steals time from the company. What he claims to be and what he really is just don't have any connection."

Man would throw the bums out of the church, but God will not allow it. The farmer in the parable replied, "No; lest in gathering the weeds you root up the wheat along with them." Why should we not try to get rid of these unworthy folks? Well, who is to throw whom out? Who is to judge who is a sinner or a hypocrite? Are we Christians not all sinners? Jesus taught, "Judge not that you be not judged." Are we not all sinners in terms of degree? Some are greater sinners than others. The sin of pride is as bad as the sin of adultery. Though not all are guilty of adultery, who is not guilty of pride?

The farmer in the parable said we should not weed the field because we would do more harm than good. You will pull up the good wheat with the weeds. When we try to drive out sinners from the church, we usually drive out some good people at the same time. The offender has family and friends who may not be guilty. Out of love for the offender, these good people will go with him to show their loyalty. A public trial of an offender stirs up the church, offends many, and people take sides. The church is left in turmoil, weaker than when the offender was in it. The offender leaves the church bitter and angry. You can be sure that he will never again come back to church. What has the church gained? It is like capital punishment: punish the criminal with death and you have no chance of rehabilitating him. Man may turn unsatisfactory people out of other areas of life, but it is not wise to do it in the church. Our ultimate goal is to win all men to repentance, and if we drive them away from us, we have lost our chance. Thus, we must be content to have weeds amid the wheat.

"Bundles to be Burned

What will God do about the nominal and weak Christians in the church? What does he propose to do with the holy tares among the wheat? In the parable, the farmer-owner says, "Let both grow together until the harvest; and at harvest time I will tell the reapers, Gather the weeds first and bind them in bundles to be burned, but gather the wheat into my barn." In the face of the shameful condition of weeds in the wheat, God shows his forbearance, his patience. He would let the weeds of immoral Christians remain in the church in the hope that they will repent. He gives them time to change to wheat before the harvest time, the end of the world, the great day of judgment.

God surely knows what he is doing and proposing, because we know that it is possible for even the worst to experience a complete change of life. When a person meets Christ, his life is often turned completely around.

This happened to a Saul turned into a Paul. It was the case with John Newton, from a captain of a slave to a hymn-writer, "Amazing Grace." In our time it happened to Eldridge Cleaver, a former black militant and Communist, who became a Black Muslim. He spent time in San Quentin prison for rape and robbery. He helped found the Black Panther Party and was involved in a shoot-out with police. In 1975 while in exile in France, he had a conversion experience. The day after this experience with Christ he decided to return to America, give himself up to the FBI, and face trial. Now he is appearing on TV telling the country what Christ can do for one's life. He turned from a weed to wheat.

Should we as faithful church members adopt the stance of God in regard to sinners? Instead of thinking of driving them out of the church, would it not be more Christian not to criticize or condemn sinners, but to pray for them and their conversion? It would be better for us to take the role of the Prodigal's father and wait and long for the wayward to return home.

But, there is an end to God's patience. The sinner in the church does not have eternity. He has only time, and that time will come to an end at harvest time. In the parable Jesus teaches that the wicked in the church will be gathered in bundles and burned: destroyed, annihilated. This seems like a hard word, but it is true. Jesus preached, "Repent or you will perish." In John 3:16 it is explained that God gave Jesus that no one should *perish* but have everlasting life. Sin must be annihilated. God is God, and he will have the victory over sin, Satan, and death. The time is coming when all evil and evil-doers will be consumed.

Yet, when this takes place, in a sense God will be defeated. It is not his purpose that any one person should be lost. He desires that all shall be saved. But what can God do if there are those who will not repent and be saved? They send themselves to the fire of the weeds. Let it be crystal clear: God does not want you to die. God wants you to live and live forever. That is why he gave his only son to die on the cross: to keep you from the fires of hell. God really loves you and wants you to live forever.

The church is like no other organization or institution. Unlike all other groups, it embraces both the good and the bad, wheat and weeds, the hypocrites and the sincere. The reason is that the church is of God and he tolerates inferior Christians with patience until harvest time. You can be sure that the church is of God, for only because God is in it and works through it, the church exists century after century and does a magnificent amount of good in the world in spite of the sorry kind of people in the church. Until the end of time the church will always have holy tares in it, and these tares hold back the progress of the church in saving the world. The church, right now, needs more wheat and less tares. But, never forget, there is a reckoning day, and each must answer the question: When the harvest time comes, when God makes his final judgment upon you, will you be found in a burning bundle of holy tares, or gathered safe in heaven's barn?

Not For Sale at Any Price
Pentecost X

*"Again, the kingdom of heaven is like a merchant in
search of fine pearls, who, on finding one pearl of great
value, went and sold all that he had and bought it."*
[*Matthew 13:45-46*]

Before you answer this question, think deeply for a
minute. What is your most valuable possession? What is
so valuable to you that if someone would want to buy it,
you would say, "It's not for sale at any price"? The
person who answers like that is saying to the prospective
buyer that the article is considered so valuable that no
amount of money could buy it. Do you have such a
possession that is beyond price? Is it a jewel — an
heirloom — a book — a person? That must have been the
way the merchant in our text felt after he sold all to buy
the pearl of great value. He found a jewel that was worth
more than all his other possessions. He would not sell
that pearl at any price. Jesus says this is the way it is
with the kingdom of heaven. It is worth more than all
your possessions. To get it a person would be willing to
sell all his other possessions to buy it. For a Christian,
then, the kingdom of heaven is the maximum value, the
summum bonum, the ultimate in worth. Could you say
that the kingdom of heaven is your pearl of great price,
the most precious possession you have? If you have it,
would you say to a prospective buyer, "Not for sale at
any price?" If not, how, you may ask, do I come to that
point about the kingdom?

A Judge of Values

To get the pearl of the kingdom of heaven you need to
be able to recognize value when you see it. Our text says
that the merchant found "one pearl of great value." This

pearl merchant was in the business of dealing with pearls. If he was going to find the pearl of greatest value, he would have to be able to judge the value of pearls. From our own experience we know that pearls are of different values. There is the simulated pearl which may fool you by appearing to be genuine. A better quality of pearl is the cultured pearl resulting from putting a grain of sand in an oyster. The best pearl is the natural pearl, very rare and very precious. Among natural pearls, some are better than others according to size and color. A genuine pearl can be costly. It is said that Cleopatra had two pearls, each worth $400,000.

Our problem is recognizing value when we see it. A few years ago the largest known existing diamond was found. It weighs almost half a pound and is valued at $11.7 million. It was found on a conveyor belt in a diamond-processing plant in West Africa. The unpolished gem was the size of a hen's egg and resembled a lump of frosted glass. If someone had not recognized it as a diamond instead of a chunk of glass, it may have been forever lost. Likewise, an executor sold a grandfather clock along with the furnishings of a widower who left no children. The clock was about thirty years old and was not working. It was sold for $100. It cost the buyer $200 to put the clock into a running condition and to get the chimes working. The clock repairman estimated that the foreign-made works were worth $6,000 on today's market, the cabinet was worth at least $1,000, and the three sets of chimes would bring the total value of the clock to $12,000. What a bargain for the buyer — a $12,000 article for $100! How do you think the seller will feel when he learns that he sold the clock for the price of junk when he really had a jewel on his hands?

One of our problems today is not only that we do not recognize true values but that we have mixed-up values. We have our prices mixed. One time a prankster got into a hardware store and rearranged the price tags on the articles in the window. The next day the manager of the store learned that he was offering single nails at $10 each while hammers were priced at five cents each. A hand-saw was priced at $150 while a power saw was listed at $15. We seem to have our values turned upside down.

This confusion of values can be seen in the salaries that are paid. In New York a policeman earns over $19,000 per year. A San Francisco street-cleaner gets $17,000 annually. An average Atlanta truck driver earns $21,000 a year. A baseball pitcher is hired on a million dollar contract. Joe Namath rejected an offer of $500,000 for three years of playing football, a $500,000 bonus, and $100,000 annually for the first twenty years of retirement. Barbara Walters went from NBC to ABC to get a salary of one million dollars annually to report the evening news on ABC-TV. In contrast, we pay secretaries, pastors, teachers, nurses, and other service personnel a wage just above poverty level. We show what our values are by the price we are willing to pay.

Our values are mixed up when it comes to material and spiritual values. Many of us put material possessions and our financial income as top values in our lives. We eat, live, struggle, and fight for ever larger incomes. The economic aspect is more important than moral considerations. Some would even eat money if they could. Physicians at a New York hospital removed more than three hundred coins from the stomach of a thirty-eight-year-old man. X-rays showed that he swallowed quarters, dimes, nickels, and pennies. Not many would go that far, but we still place such high value on money that we would do almost anything at any price to get more of it.

Our values are mixed up when it comes to human values as against material values. We tend to treat people as things and things as people. A pastor tells of living on the farm when he was a boy. They had a jeep which had a problem with the brakes. One day he took his brother and two-year-old sister for a ride along with a puppy dog. As they were riding along something happened to the steering. He slammed on the brakes but they did not work. As they headed for a ditch, he called to his brother, "Grab the baby!" When the jeep came to a stop, he found a few scratches on his sister and his brother with the bulldog in his arms perfectly safe! Is this a sample of our priorities: dogs before people? The same was brought out in the case of a woman in New Guinea who came to a mission hospital to get her finger bandaged. It is the custom there to amputate a joint of a finger to express grief when a loved one dies. As the doctor was bandaging the finger, he expressed sorrow and asked who died. Through an interpreter he learned that the lady's pig died! She loved her pig as much, if not more, than a member of the family.

What are our values when it comes to choosing our heroes? Who is the greatest person of history? Whom do we emulate as great? The Tussaud Wax Works of London released figures on their 1976 poll of visitors' favorite heroes and heroines. The number one person was Joan of Arc. Second was Churchill. In third place were John Kennedy, Jesus, and Admiral Nelson. Jesus is in third place and even there he must share the level with two others. Doesn't that say something about what we consider to be of most value?

In today's first lesson we heard about God's asking Solomon, the new king, what he wanted most of all. Wisely, Solomon asked not for riches or power but wisdom to rule aright. When it comes to our being able to judge true values, the real pearl compared with inferior pearls of life, we need to follow Solomon's example and ask God for wisdom to know good from bad, to know the better from the good. Unless we can judge true value, how can we make the kingdom of heaven the top value of our lives?

In Search of the Best

Assuming that we have the wisdom to know true values, our next step must be to find the top value in life. Our text tells us that the pearl merchant was "in search of fine pearls." For him, it was a lifelong search. Day by day he looked at pearls, sizing them up, passing judgment on them in the hope of someday finding the very best pearl.

If we are going to find the pearl of the kingdom of heaven, we, too, must be in search of it. To look for the pearl means you and I will be open and receptive to what we want. Jesus enunciated this principle when he taught: "Ask and you will receive, seek and you will find, knock and it will be opened to you." Solomon received wisdom because this was his greatest desire. If we keep an open mind and a receptive spirit, one day we will find what we are looking for. It may come unexpectedly or suddenly. In the middle of the night, a great preacher, Horace Bushnell, shouted, "I found it! I found it!" This awakened his wife and she asked impatiently, "What did you find?" He replied, "I have found the gospel!" He might have said, "I have found the pearl of the kingdom of heaven."

The thing to remember is that the pearl may not be found in a day or a week. The pearl merchant in the text was looking for the supreme pearl for years and then he found it — at last! This may mean a lifetime search, but we must never give up; we must keep searching until we find it. The pearl may be found where you do not expect it. Years ago there lived a man who was restless for wealth. He sold his beautiful farm in South Africa to go in search of diamonds and gold. He traveled from country to country. He followed every clue, but found nothing. In despair and broken health, he threw himself into a river and drowned. The man who bought his farm was walking over the land one day and stepped across a stream. Something caught his eye. He bent down and diamond. He found one, then another. On that farm there was the richest diamond field in the world. The kingdom of heaven might be right where you live, right where you worship or work.

If you are going to look for something, you must first know what you want to find. How can you find something if you do not know what you are looking for? According to our text, we are saying we want to find the pearl of the kingdom of heaven. What is that? We do not understand "kingdom" because we live in a democracy. At present we are not interested in heaven. We want to go there some day but not just right now! To have the kingdom of heaven is a life in God, with God, and for God. It is that kind of life, that puts heaven on earth. We live in a happy relationship with God as a child of God, and we live according to his will. It is a realm of moral and spiritual values. When we find the kingdom of heaven, we receive as by-products certain qualities of life. First we seek the Kingdom and these values are given to us.

What are we talking about? To be in the kingdom of heaven is to be happy here and now. In 1977, the popular TV star of "Chico and the Man," Freddie Prinze, committed suicide at age twenty-two. He had everything to live for: youth, a million dollar contract with a Las Vegas night club, and one of the highest status roles in his work. Though millions laughed with him on his shows, he was unhappy. In his despondency he would ask, "Where do I fit in? Where is my happiness?" When he was told that his happiness was in being a star, he sadly said, "No, that's not happiness for me anymore." Happiness is to be found in getting the kingdom of heaven, for in that kingdom happiness is in serving God and bringing happiness to others through service. The true Christian is the happiest person in the world.

To have the kingdom of heaven is to have peace of mind and heart. This peace the world does not have and cannot give. Gary Gilmore, the first to be executed for two murders in ten years, spent sleepless nights in prison, haunted by ghosts. He explained, "They're slippery, sneaky, and get tangled in your hair like bats . . . demons with dirty, furry bodies whispering vile things . . . creeping, crawling, red-eyed soulless beasts. They bite and claw, scratch, and screech." The person with the kingdom is saved from this kind of inner hell. For the one in the kingdom of heaven there is the peace that results from being one with God by faith in Christ.

The kingdom of heaven is also a condition of love. According to Paul, Christian love is the greatest thing in the world, the *summum bonum*. Here is the pearl of great value. Without love nothing else really counts or matters. A million dollar mansion without love is worth less than a lean-to. Nothing can match the value of having one say to you, "I could not live without you" or "I'd die for you." Do you have any one who says that to you? If you do, you have a taste of the kingdom of heaven. It is a kingdom of love, a love that paid the full price of death on a cross. That love of God is our chief treasure.

Buy the Best

Suppose now that you have found the great pearl of the kingdom and you knew that it was the real thing, what would you do about it? What did the pearl merchant in the text do about it? Our text says, he "went and sold all that he had and bought it." This means that he realized that the value of this one jewel was worth more than all of his other pearls and all his possessions. The pearl was worth selling all in order to buy it. This is a natural response. It is the logical and sensible thing to do. This has been the universal response of Christians to finding the kingdom. When the Disciples found the pearl in Jesus, "They left everything and followed him." When Paul found Christ, he wrote, "Indeed I count everything as loss because of the surpassing worth of knowing

Christ Jesus my Lord. For his sake I have suffered the loss of all things, and count them as refuse . . . that I may know him . . ." When St. Francis gave his life to Christ, before an assembled court, he took off all his clothes and gave them to his father. To avoid embarrassment, the bishop put his robe around the naked body of Francis. He literally gave all to have Christ. When a person finds the kingdom of heaven, his former values and honors turn into dust before the excellency of Christ. In *The Old Rugged Cross* we sing this truth, "So I'll cherish the old rugged cross, till my trophies at last I lay down."

Like the merchant, we want to buy this great pearl. To get it we sell all that we have because it is worth it. This is done voluntarily. We do not sell all out of a sense of duty. Nobody needs to pressure us to do it. We do it on our own free will and accord. We do it because we want to do it. We are convinced of its value and we want it more than anything else in the whole world. Having the best, we are no longer interested in second best. It is like a young man who has many girl friends. One day he meets the girl of his dreams. For him she gathers up all the qualities of the other girls. This is the pearl of great price to him. Nobody needs to suggest to him that he stop seeing the other girls. Now he is not interested in being with anyone but *the* girl.

It gets down to a matter of relative values. The merchant sells his other pearls to buy the best pearl. These other pearls are not bad, nor worthless. They have a certain value. Because he found something far better, he sells the inferior items. This is the way it works out for a Christian in getting the kingdom of heaven. He does not say that everything but God's Kingdom is bad, but he finds the best in Christ. Take the matter of money. Money in itself is not evil. It is very necessary. You need money to buy groceries, to purchase clothing, to pay the utilities, and to meet the mortgage payments. You must have money to stay alive. For the Christian, however, money is not everything; it is not the highest value in life. It is secondary to the riches of the grace of Christ. There are things more valuable than money, things money cannot buy: friendship, love, honor, respect, faith, hope. Money is "sold" to a subordinate position to get the kingdom of heaven.

Apply this to the field of religion. We are living in a pluralistic age of many faiths. A Christian does not say that all other religions are bad, but he does say that Christianity is the very best, worth more than all the others put together. In 1977, during one week in January, ten million Hindus dipped themselves into the Ganges River. They traveled from all parts of India to bathe in the river for the washing away of their sins. At this special festival adherents are promised the benefit of escape from the endless cycle of birth and rebirth by entering into union with the Absolute. There may be some value in this because probably some will find release and peace. That is fine as far as it goes. Contrast this with the gospel that tells us that Christ died for our sins and only his blood can cleanse the soul of sin. No physical water has the power to wash away the stains of sin. Only the precious blood of God in Christ can erase guilt from the heart. This is the purpose of Christian missions to non-Christian people: to acquaint them with a better way to get right with God by faith in Christ.

To have the kingdom of heaven does not necessarily mean that you must sell all and embrace total poverty, but it means material things must come second to the kingdom. To have the pearl of great price does not mean the ascetic life in which you deny youself every pleasure. No, it means you can in moderation eat, drink, and be merry as long as it is subordinated to the Kingdom of God. It does not mean that you must live a life imprisoned in "Don'ts" with strict legalism and Puritanism. To be a Christian is to be free to live according to the spirit of the law. Yet, this liberty is put under the lordship of Christ so that our liberty does not become lawless license. In the Sermon on the Mount,

Jesus summed it up, "Seek first the kingdom of God and all these things shall be added to you." Put the Kingdom first in your life and all other things will be placed in a subordinate position to Christ. This is what it means to sell all you have to buy the pearl of great value.

In a church bulletin, a typographical error was made in announcing a hymn: "Wise up, O men of God." That could very well be the message for us. Why don't you and I wise up and be through with lesser things in life? The greatest value, the top good, the ultimate of worth is the kingdom of heaven. Wise up and then rise up to embrace the pearl of great value, Jesus Christ our Lord.

Food for Faith
Pentecost XI

*Now when Jesus heard this, he withdrew from there in a
boat to a lonely place apart. But when the crowds heard
it, they followed him on foot from the towns. As he went
ashore he saw a great throng; and he had compassion on
them, and healed their sick. When it was evening, the
disciples came to him and said, "This is a lonely place,
and the day is now over; send the crowds away to go into
the villages and buy food for themselves." Jesus said,
"They need not go away; you give them something to
eat." They said to him, "We have only five loaves here
and two fish." And he said, "Bring them here to me."
Then he ordered the crowds to sit down on the grass;
and taking the five loaves and the two fish he looked up
to heaven, and blessed, and broke and gave the loaves to
the disciples, and the disciples gave them to the crowds.
And they all ate and were satisfied. And they took up
twelve baskets full of the broken pieces left over. And
those who ate were about five thousand men, besides
women and children." [Matthew 14:13-21]*

In a fashionable Manhattan church, as the sermon
came to an end, the pastor announced the closing hymn
and urged people to come forward during the singing of
the hymn to accept Christ. A little pinched girl in poor
clothing slipped into the back of the church and heard the
pastor's appeal to come forward. She responded and
walked down to the front. When she reached the
minister, she timidly said, "I am hungry." While people
were urged to come for spiritual food, one came for
physical food. Here are the two basic needs of a person:
bread for the body and bread for the soul. An oriental
proverb is right: "If you have two pennies, spend one for
bread and the other for flowers." Though man does not

live by bread alone, he cannot live without bread. In our text dealing with the feeding of the five thousand, these two basic breads come together. Jesus, the spiritual bread of life, gives physical bread to the hungry. Today these two needs are foremost in the world. Can Jesus still meet those needs? If so, how?

Hunger is Real

Jesus today can supply bread for the world's body. As it was at the time of the miracle in our text, hunger is a reality. Crowds of people came to the country, to a lonely place, to hear Jesus preach and to be healed. The Disciples knew the people were hungry but there was no place for them to get food. Thus, they say to Jesus, "Send the crowds away to go into the villages and buy food for themselves." Today there are more than five thousand times five thousand who are in a lonely place and cannot buy bread. It is not news to say that we are in a crisis of world hunger. It is said that we breathe twenty times in one minute. That is exactly how many people in the world die from hunger in a minute. One dies each time we take a breath! It is reported that four hundred sixty million people are hungry. Because of the population explosion, two hundred thousand new mouths must be fed *each day*. It seems as though a greater miracle than the feeding of the five thousand is needed if today's people are going to have sufficient bread.

What can we as individuals do about this difficult and complex world problem? Before we can do anything, we must possess the quality Jesus had as he looked upon the sick and hungry crowd. "He had compasson on them," says the text. Here is the key to doing something. Where there is a heart, there is a way! Do we as individuals really care that half of the world's people are undernourished? If we cared, we would obey Jesus' command to the Disciples, "You give them something to eat."

One thing we can do to feed the physically hungry is to conserve our food that we might have more to share with the hungry of the world . . . Americans are guilty of wasting food. It is said that school children waste twenty-five percent of their food by leaving that amount on their plates. In one school ten gallons of milk was poured down the drain because children left that amount in their glasses during lunch. Think of how many children in other parts of the world would grab left-overs for just a taste! Some time ago we had a graduate student from India in our home for dinner. He brought his wife and children to live here while he worked for his doctor's degree. A full glass of milk was set before the little boy. He was amazed at the full glass and asked his father how much of it he could drink. Later his father explained to us that in India they could have but one glass of milk to be divided among all the children, and each could drink only so much of the milk in order to leave the rest for the other children. The little fellow could not believe he was going to have a whole glass of milk for himself! How much food do you leave on your plate when dinner is over? Could those left-overs keep someone from starving?

Also, we waste so much sometimes by strikes. In 1976 thirty thousand workers in twenty-eight California canneries went on strike for three weeks. The result was that fifteen percent of that year's crop of peaches, five percent of the tomatoes, and thirty percent of the apricots rotted while hungry people died for lack of food.

What can we do about world hunger? We can share our food by eating less. Experts tell us that we are eating ourselves to death by over-eating. Obesity is America's number one health problem. The average American eats daily nine hundred more calories than he needs. It is reported that fifty percent of us are overweight. Fifty-three percent of the deaths are caused by diseases that are related to obesity. We Americans spend annually ten billion dollars on diets and slimming programs. Even our dogs are over-fed. A recent report says that forty-one percent of American dogs are overweight. This is causing dog food companies to offer diet food for dogs such as "Fit and Trim" which claims to have less calories for your dog. Look at the miserable contrast: the overfilled stomachs of dogs almost touching the ground and the bloated stomachs of children suffering from malnutrition! If we had compassion on the poor and hungry, we would voluntarily change our life-styles which would call for less food in-take. Then, we could take the money saved from buying less food and give it to our church's program to send food abroad to the destitute. One denomination within a two-year period gave eight million dollars for world hunger. This was possible because loyal members sacrificed by eating less that others might eat more.

The problem of world hunger is not in having enough bread for the world's population. Christ took five loaves and two fish and stretched them until the five thousand had more than enough. The generosity of God's provisions is fantastic. The hunger problem is basically one of distribution. Jesus gave the bread to the Disciples to distribute to the people. In our day those who have, as America does, should have the compassion of Jesus to share with those who have little or no food.

Soul Food

The problem of world hunger cannot be overstated, but there is a greater hunger in the world than the hunger for physical food. It is the hunger for spiritual food, food for the soul. God, through the words of Amos, said, "I will send a famine on the land; not a famine of bread . . . but a famine of hearing the words of the Lord." Once John Wesley advised, "Do justice to your soul. Do not starve yourself any longer." On the surface it may not seem as though our text deals with this kind of bread. Scholars tell us that this account of the feeding of the five thousand is closely related to the Eucharist. It seems like a re-enactment of the Last Supper: "Taking the five loaves and the two fish he looked up to heaven, and blessed, and broke and gave the loaves to the disciples . . ." This is the only miracle given by all four Gospels, and there are six accounts of it. This shows how important the miracle of bread was to the early Christians. In the weekly Lord's Supper, they had a re-enactment of this miracle of Jesus' feeding the people. In the Eucharist Jesus again took bread, blessed it, and broke it for distribution to the Disciples for the nourishment of their souls.

Just as physical hunger is a very real fact of life, spiritual hunger is just as real. There are many millions more who are spiritually malnourished, and multitudes are dying of spiritual starvation. Many of these are overfed, overweight people with stuffed bellies but with anemic souls. On a physical level we can see the hunger's reality in bloated stomachs, protruding ribs, and pinched faces. Likewise, there are symptoms of spiritual hunger here and all over the world.

We see today spiritually hungry people who are going outside the church for soul food. This is a judgment upon the church for apparently not satisfying the spiritual needs of the people. Forty-two million Americans, for instance, or one out of every five, has espoused astrology. They believe that the position of the stars has something to do with their daily lives. Two-thirds of our newspapers carry a daily horoscope. Eight out of every ten Americans can tell you under what star they were born. This turning to astrology is an indication that people are looking for something transcendant; they are looking for guidance from a force beyond themselves. Six million Americans have embraced Transcendental Meditation and thirty thousand new people each month are signing up for instruction. This points to a need for meditation to get in touch with God, something many church people must feel they are not getting now. Add to this number five million people who are seeking union with God by Yoga. Three million Americans belong to the charismatic movement, a desire for an experience with the Spirit. Many of these charismatics claim that the average church is cold and lacking in spiritual warmth. Add to this various heretical sects that are attracting people by the tens of thousands: Scientology and the Unification church by Moon.

Why are many people spiritually hungry today? One reason is they are trying to exist on "junk food." Teen-agers are accused of eating this kind of food — odds and ends: cokes and hot dogs and hamburgers and french fries. They may be filling but they lack the vitamins and balanced diet that the body needs. A lot of us are trying to live on spiritual junk food. What goes into our minds and hearts? What is feeding our spirits? Many Americans get their food from TV. It is reported that the average child sees twenty-three hours of TV per week. By the time a child reaches age eighteen, he sees twenty-three thousand hours of TV, equivalent to three years of his life. And what do they get on TV, what feeds their minds and hearts? They are fed materialism through the constant appearance of commercials, often six at a time. In 1976 it is said that TV stations ran three hundred thirty-five thousand commercials per month! In these commercials we are fed with a materialistic view of life. We are told that things make life happy and worthwhile. Buy, buy, and you will have all the good things in life. On the other hand, TV is feeding us with violence, with more of it coming each year. By the time a child reaches age eighteen, it is claimed that he has seen eighteen thousand murders. On children's TV cartoons, an act of violence is shown at the rate of one per minute. These scenes of violence are sowing the seeds of hatred, brutality, and revenge in the minds of people.

The tragedy of our times is that we are content to feed our souls with crackers when we could be getting a spiritual banquet. We are living on chaff and husks rather than the good meat of a steak. Once an immigrant came across the Atlantic on a ship. Because of the lack of money, he decided not to go to the dining room and pay high prices for food but rather eat from a package of crackers. After some days, the crackers did not satisfy. He went to the restaurant and asked the head waiter what it would cost to get a meal. He was told that the meals were free, for they were included in his ticket. He could have had seven-course meals four times a day, but he was satisfied with crackers. Many today are just as foolish and stupid by feeding their souls on things that do not satisfy or nourish when they could be eating at the Master's banquet table several times a day.

Hungry for What?

When we talk about spiritual hunger, what do we mean? When we are physically hungry, no one needs to tell us that we are hungry. But do we know when we have spiritual hunger pains? Sometimes we are starving in spirit and do not realize it. Wonder why God did not give us spiritual hunger pains like he gave us pains in the stomach? One of our spiritual hungers is the desire for security. After the Second World War, thousands of refugees were fed and cared for in Allied camps. However, at night they could not sleep. They were restless and afraid. Someone got an idea to give them a piece of bread to take with them to bed. It was not to be eaten, just held. This produced marvelous results. The children went to sleep in the security that they would have something to eat the next day. It gave them a sense of security and peace. Without God we are insecure and afraid of the darkness of the world. If we had the Bread of Life, we would feel secure.

Our spiritual hunger takes the form of needing love and friendship. Some time ago there was a youth wearing a T-shirt with this legend: "Luv Me." This is the cry of many, many people who do not wear T-shirts but whose hearts are crying out with loneliness. When Rupert Brooks was about to sail for Europe, he noticed a crowd of people waiting for the ship to depart. He could see that they would be waving to their loved ones on the ship. But he had no one to wave to him. He went down the gangplank and found a young lad. He offered to pay the lad if he would just wave his handkerchief to him when the ship left. The boy agreed, and later when the ship pulled away, Brooks looked down and saw a grubby hand wave a handkerchief at him. In our spiritual starvation, we would even pay to have someone show a little friendliness. We are starved for love.

As Christ in the miracle provided bread for the physically hungry and still does today through his disciples' sharing, he provides bread for the soul of man. He does not only provide the bread but he *is* the Bread. In providing physical bread, he performs a miracle by multiplying the loaves and fish, but in providing spiritual bread he performs the miracle of giving himself to us as the Bread of Life. He preached that he was the living bread from heaven. If anyone ate this bread, he would live forever. Jesus is the Bread and we satisfy our hunger and gain spiritual strength when we eat him. He who eats my flesh and drinks my blood, Jesus said, gets eternal life.

How do you eat this Bread of life? How do you eat Jesus Christ? How do you digest the Son of God? One way is by maintaining daily private devotions. It is a time spent alone with Christ, apart from the family and the busyness of the day. It is a secret tryst with Christ to feed on him. This sounds like figurative language. How does one do this in actuality? It means taking some time — five, ten, fifteen, or twenty minutes — each day to spend in the presence of Christ, the Bread of Life. You ask, "What do I do for the period? Look at the wall? Daydream?" No, you take your Bible and read a passage until you have found something that speaks to you. Now stop and reflect on what you read. Is God saying anything to you in this passage? Any command to obey? Any promise to claim? Any example to follow? Any sin to avoid? Any prayer to echo? This is called reflection or meditation. You get quiet and still. You focus your mind on God and his Word. The next step is to respond to God by prayer which is talking to him. Speak to him as you do to a friend in conversation. Tell him everything and ask him for what you may need for that day. By doing this day in and day out, you will be feeding your soul with the Bread of Life. You will grow strong within. Your faith will mature.

You can eat the Bread of Life also in public worship. You gather where fellow-believers join hearts and voices in praising God and listening to his Word taught and preached in a church service. Since Christ is the heart and center of the Bible, we can say that the Bible is the Bread of Life. When the Bible is preached, the pastor is breaking the Bread of Life for us. Christians feed on the Word of God as they hear it in church. In 1976, a representative of the Lutheran World Federation published a report of a recent visit to Lutheran congregations in Russia. He found among them a deep hunger for the Bread of Life. In a congregation of eight hundred adult members, nine hundred were present for the church service. Their service lasted from 10 a.m. until four p.m. He reported about the preaching, "It was as if the people could not get enough." The Russians said they did not like modern sermons because they were too short. They wanted sermons to go no less than an hour. Does this put our current craze for eight minute sermons to shame?

The fullest meal of Bread comes in the Lord's Supper, the Eucharist. Here Jesus comes in the bread and wine to be with us — physically, specifically, concretely. He says to us as we kneel at the altar, "This is my body . . . This is my blood." We really and truly receive him by faith, and our souls feed on him. We become one with him. In that union we find peace and joy.

In 1972 a chartered plane flew from Montevideo for Chile. It carried fifteen members of a rugby team, along with twenty-five others. The plane crashed into the side of the Andes mountains. Only sixteen of the forty-five survived by eating the flesh of the dead passengers. Two of the team set out to find some help. They struggled across huge mountains and after many days came across a peasnt keeping watch over his flock in a remote valley of the Andes. At first the farmer thought the two men were terrorists and left them. The next morning he was back and the two survivors frantically tried to make him understand but the roar of a river separating them would not let them converse. A message tied to a rock was thrown across the river explaining who they were. In return, the farmer cut off a piece of bread, tied it around a stone, and threw it across the river. The two men held the bread in their hands. The one turned to his friend and said, "We are saved." The other replied, "Yes, we are saved." This is what physical bread does: it saves from starvation. This is what the Bread of Life does: it saves from spiritual death. Every person needs both kinds of bread to be saved. O Thou Bread of Life, give us this Bread that we may live!

Jesus Makes House Calls
Pentecost XII

Then he made the disciples get into the boat and go before him to the other side, while he dismissed the crowds. And after he had dismissed the crowds, he went up into the hills by himself to pray. When evening came, he was there alone, but the boat by this time was many furlongs distant from the land, beaten by the waves; for the wind was against them. And in the fourth watch of the night he came to them, walking on the sea. But when the disciples saw him walking on the sea, they were terrified, saying, "It is a ghost!" And they cried out for fear. But immediately he spoke to them, saying, "Take heart, it is I; have no fear."

And Peter answered him, 'Lord, if it is you, bid me come to you on the water." He said, "Come." So Peter got out of the boat and walked on the water, and came to Jesus; but when he saw the wind, he was afraid, and beginning to sink he cried out, "Lord, save me." Jesus immediately reached out his hand and caught him, saying to him, "O man of little faith, why did you doubt?" And when they got into the boat, the wind ceased. And those in the boat worshiped him, saying, "Truly you are the Son of God." [Matthew 14:22-33]

The day of professional people's making house calls is just about over. If you want service, usually you must go to their offices. It may still be possible to get house calls if you are in dire need. How do you get firemen to come to your home? Only when your house is on fire! How do you get the police to come to your house? Only when we report a crime such as a break-in. How do you get a physician to come to your home? If he comes at all, you must be so sick that you cannot make it to his office. In each case, someone will come to your house only if you are in need or in trouble.

When a person is in need, Jesus, too, makes house calls. He will come to you when you need him. This fact was demonstrated in today's Gospel lesson concerning Jesus' walk on the water. Jesus had been teaching and healing all day. He felt the need of being alone to pray. He sent the people away and told the disciples to get into a boat and go to the other side of the Sea of Galilee. On the trip across the sea a storm came up, the wind was against them, and paddling the boat was futile. Jesus must have sensed their need of him. He left his prayers to go to their rescue. Not having a boat, Jesus walked on the water to them. What a strange house call that was! The disciples' house was a boat. And consider the time the call was made — three o'clock in the morning! This is just like Jesus: he comes to us any place, at any time, to help us in our need.

When There Is Need

Let us put this down to where you and I live. "Will Jesus come to my house?" you may ask. Our text tells us that he will come when you are in need of him. Jesus appeared to the disciples when they were in trouble and in need of Jesus. "And in the fourth watch of the night, he came to them, walking on the sea." This is typical of God throughout the history of his people. When the Israelites were suffering in slavery at the hands of the Egyptians, God came to Moses and called him to go back to Egypt and free the people. In today's First Lesson we heard about Elijah's flight to a cave in a wilderness because he was afraid of Queen Jezebel. In his need of overcoming his despair, God came to him to cheer him up and send him on his way. After the resurrection, two disciples were on their way to Emmaus and were despondent because they had hoped that Jesus would have redeemed the nation. Jesus came to them and revealed himself in the breaking of bread. It means that God loves his people and when they are in trouble or need of any kind, he comes and makes a house call.

Isn't this the way it is with those who love others? If a friend is in need, we go immediately to see if there is anything we can do to help out. When a child is sick, a mother hovers over her child. When a wife has a car accident, a husband usually races to the scene to see if his wife is OK. When a son is put in jail, a father runs to post bail. When a member of the family has an operation, the hospital room is usually occupied by a member of the family to express love and concern. If there is a death in the family, relatives drop everything to be on hand to comfort. This is done out of love and compassion. Since God loves us more than any human being can possibly love, God and his Son make haste to come to us in our situation.

Common Needs

Jesus could not wait to come to the disciples who were caught in a storm on the sea. He did not have time to walk along the shore and borrow a boat to get to the men. For the first time, he walked on the water, not to astound people but to help his friends in trouble. Just as the disciples were in a bad situation, we find our situation to be often similar to theirs. You will note that the disciples were alone. Jesus had gone to the mountain top to pray. He was probably miles away from the boat filled with men. The text tells us they were many furlongs distant from the land. There were no other boats nearby to help them. They were *alone*.

There are times when we, too, are alone and need Christ to come to our house. Like the Prodigal son, we get independent and rebellious. We decide we are going to go our own way in life. We think we know it all and we leave home and friends to make it on our own. The time comes when our new friends forsake us and we come to the point of being all alone as the Prodigal was. A sinful life is a lonely life. Or, it may be that we leave home for marriage. We may have married someone our family did not approve because they feared we would not make it together. Nevertheless, we were sure we loved each other and love could surmount any obstacle. Then in a few years troubles mutliply. A spouse cannot go home now. He or she cannot ask parents what to do. To divorce or not to divorce no one can answer; in his/her aloneness he/she must face the problem. Again, there is an aloneness when we face an operation that may be terminal. No one can die for us. No one can face our Maker for us. When the jaws of death open before us, we are so all alone.

It is at such a time of loneliness, like the disciples on the sea, that Christ comes to us. God came to Moses when he was alone on the hills tending sheep. Jacob was alone when he wrestled with an angel. Elijah was alone in a cave when God came not in the fire, wind, or the earthquake but in the still small voice. In Gethsemane Jesus went beyond the three disciples to be alone to struggle with God about the cross. If Jesus is not close to us, it may be because we are very, very busy, running here and there. Euripides once wrote, "Even Zeus cannot reveal himself to a busybody." It is when we withdraw to a solitary place and we dwell in solitude that Christ comes to us. Do you reserve a period of time daily to be alone for Christ to come to you?

Jesus came to the house-boat of the disciples in the darkest hour of the night. It was the fourth watch of the night, about 3 a.m. You know how dark it is at this time of night! Many of us have such dark nights of life. There is no light of hope. We are filled with the darkness of doubt, despair, and despondency. It is so dark that we can see no way out, no hope of anything better. For some the darkness is so thick that suicide is the only answer. Recently a survey was made of one thousand High

School students in Oregon, conducted by the Governor's Commission on Youth. The study revealed that forty percent said they considered suicide and six percent said they tried to take their lives. In early 1977, Freddie Prinze, a popular TV star, took his life at age twenty-two. It is said that the reason for this tragic act was that he felt he had no place in this world. If only Freddie had realized that Jesus was standing by to help him! Jesus would have given a reason for living and would have explained the meaning of life. When we are in the darkest hours of our lives, Jesus hastens to our side.

Note, too, that the disciples on the sea, according to our text, were frustrated. They were in the middle of the sea, far from shore. The winds were against them, for remember they had only a sailboat and were dependent on a favorable wind to get to their destination. They may have taken to the oars, but the wind was stronger than they were. They were stuck, frustrated, unable to make headway. In their helplessness Jesus comes to their house-boat.

Many of us are in the same predicament. We are frustrated. Our efforts to get somewhere are in vain. We do not know what to do or where to go. What is the solution to a particular problem of life? This is true not only with individuals like you and me but with society as a whole. In late 1976 the church called a symposium on "The Nature of a Humane Society" in Philadelphia. Seven specialists were invited to discuss current issues. They agreed that the patient is in serious trouble but not all had a cure. Those who did think they had the cure could not agree with each other on what was the cure. In his book *Mindstyles/Lifestyles*, Nathaniel Lande tells of making a first-hand evaluation of more than one thousand remedies for an ailing society. He calls all of the remedies "games" and "band-aids for cancer." He finally came to the conclusion that there is no secret in finding a solution to the problems of modern society.

When we are at the end of our rope, Christ comes to us with the answer. Christ has always been and still is the answer to every human problem. He is the way out of our dilemma. One time a party of Americans was going from one mission station to the next in Africa. After a while they realized there was no marked path and became alarmed that they might get lost in the jungle. Their hired guide allayed their fears when he said, "Follow me, I am the way." In the jungle of our pathless waste, Jesus says, "I am the way."

There is another point where Jesus comes to us as seen in his coming to the disciples on the boat. They were scared to death. They were afraid that the storm would sink the boat and they would drown. They were even more frightened when they saw a "ghost" walking on the water. These men were grown, hardened men and not easily frightened. Yet, the text tells us that they were "terrified" and "cried out for fear."

This is a common experience in our times. On a pre-Christmas visit to Manhattan a friend suggested we take a walk down the two most dangerous blocks in the city. The sidewalks were crowded with pimps and prostitutes. We saw young men and women looking at us with suspicion and threats. We were not sure that at any minute we would not be mugged. I frankly admit that I was never so scared in all my life and not for a thousand dollars would I again take the same walk! In this age of violence, many live in homes which use chaines, bolts, and extra locks for every door. We keep watch-dogs, install window bars, and purchase alarm systems. We are frightened lest we be robbed, raped, or murdered. In the midst of such fear, Christ comes to us. And to whom shall we go when we are afraid? A pastor's daughter tells about a time when a thunderstorm came during a Sunday evening church service. Her father was the pastor and her mother was the organist. During the storm the lights went out and the service came to a halt. When the lights came back on, the congregation was delighted to see her mother sitting on the lap of her father!

Ask for Help

It is true that Jesus makes a house call on us when we are in trouble or need. But, it is important to note that Jesus does not help the disciples until he is asked to help. He came walking on the water to be near them in case they would call upon him. While he was near them, the storm continued to rage. We can be thankful for this, because it means that God never imposes himself upon us. We are not cogs or slaves. He recognizes our freedom and sees us as persons. He never says, "I've come to help you. Move over and I'll take charge." This is hard for parents to remember in parent-child relationships. Parents often help children when they do not want help. As a result, the children resent the help. One child says, "Look, Mom, I want to do it myself!" It is a wise parent who makes himself/herself available but never helps unless asked. He/she gives no advice unless it is wanted.

To get help we must ask Christ for help, but we will Peter did not at first think he needed help to walk on the water. He said, "Jesus, if you can walk on water, so can I. Just ask me to come to you." He had a sense of independence and self-sufficiency, plus a measure of bravado. We today do not want help because we seem to think we do not have a problem. There is nothing wrong with us, we say; it is the other person who needs help. Or, it may be that we do not sense the need for help because we think we can handle our own problems. There may be a marriage problem. One of the couple does not think there is anything wrong, and is sure that a marriage counselor could not help. He/she feels that he/she knows as much about life as the counselor does. In my experience as a pastoral counselor, I found that many times only the wife would seek help. The husband often refused to come to discuss the marital problem. In the matter of alcoholism, it is basic that an alcoholic comes to the point where he agrees that he cannot by himself handle his problem of drinking. He must come to the point of looking to a Higher Power for deliverance. One time a mother wrote to Ann Landers about her son who went from one therapist to the next for fourteen years because she begged him to do so. None was able to help him because he thought he was smarter than all of them put together. Then the son committed suicide. With a broken heart she wrote, "He was in some ways a genius, but he just wouldn't accept help."

It may be that we realize we need help, but we are too proud to ask for it. To ask for help is an admission that someone is stronger than you are. It means you are dependent and are not self-sufficient. This is hard on the ego. There is a famous legend of Roland, one of Charlemagne's greatest warriors. Roland and his friend, Oliver, were the rearguard of Charlemagne's army. One time his little force was surrounded by the Moors. Roland had a horn that could be heard for miles. He was to blow it when in need for Charlemagne to come to his rescue. Oliver shouted to Roland, "Blow the horn!" Roland refused because he was too proud to ask for help. One by one the soldiers fell until only Oliver and Roland were left. Oliver was slain and Roland was mortally wounded. Then he blew the horn. By the time Charlemagne reached Roland, not a man was alive. He blew the horn too late.

Ask in Prayer

Christ is present when we are in trouble, when the storms of life just about undo us. He is standing by waiting to be asked for help. How do we ask for aid? Prayer is the answer, for a large part of prayer is petition. We need to come to the point Peter did when while slipping down into the sea. He cried, "Lord, save me." This is what Jesus taught us to do to get help. He said, "Ask and you shall receive." At another time, the Bible says, "You have not because you ask not." Again,

"Ask largely that your joy may be full."

If help is available for the asking, why are we so
foolish as not to ask? It may be that we do not ask in
prayer because we do not know how to pray. A New
York psychiatrist reports that in the twenty-five years of
seeing patients, he never had one who really knew how
to pray. Isn't that tragic? Could that be true with you?
Even if we do know how to ask in prayer, maybe we do
not ask because we do not believe in prayer. To have
prayers answered, it is assumed that the pray-er is one
who believes in God and that God hears and answers
prayer. Faith is a condition of prayer. Do you think your
need is only a human problem that people ought to
answer rather than go to God with it? Is it possible that
you do not believe that God can do the impossible
through prayer, or do you rely upon natural causes only
for the answer? Remember Jesus taught that with God
all things are possible.

It is one of the Christian's highest privileges just to
pray. Through prayer a believer can ask for anything
and all things, no matter how small or impossible they
may seem to be. You and I do not have to worry about
whether we are asking for the right things. It is not for
us to judge, just to ask. God will sift out our prayers and
will answer those that correspond to his will. And what
is his will? His will is our good. He will never give us
anything that will not help us. His answer is always
"yes" or "no" or "wait" or "here is a substitute." God
answers every prayer in some way that is always good
for us.

When the request is made, note how fast the answer
comes! When Peter prayed, "Lord, save me," "Jesus
immediately reached out his hand and caught him . . ."
Jesus did not take time out to think whether he would
help or not. He did not question whether Peter was
worthy of being helped. With a flash, Jesus goes to Peter
and saves him from drowning. You will note that this is
the first time Jesus does anything to help. He waits for

the request, for the cry for assistance. When we are in need Jesus comes to our house and stands by in case we need him. Then, when we call for help, when we sound the SOS, he is not on a mountain-top praying, nor is he somewhere in the heavens. He is closer than hands and feet ready to assist us. Isn't that great? How about that for good news to those in a storm of life? But, what a tragedy that we do not take everything to the Lord in prayer.

Yes, Jesus makes house calls. Our text assures us of that. Our experience confirms it. When he enters the house of our lives, his presence brings calm. "And when they got into the boat, the wind ceased." The storm was over. All were saved. The winds were like spring breezes and the waves became like ripples on a mountain lake. If you want peace of mind and calm of soul, why not ask Jesus to come into your life? He is waiting for you to ask him to come into your house-boat.

Nag, Nag, Nag!
Pentecost XIII

And Jesus went away from there and withdrew to the district of Tyre and Sidon. And behold, a Canaanite woman from that region came out and cried, "Have mercy on me, O Lord, Son of David; my daughter is severely possessed by a demon." But he did not answer her a word. And his disciples came and begged him, saying, "Send her away, for she is crying after us." He answered, "I was sent only to the lost sheep of the house of Israel." But she came and knelt before him, saying, "Lord, help me." And he answered, "It is not fair to take the children's bread and throw it to the dogs." She said, "Yes, Lord, yet even the dogs eat the crumbs that fall from their master's table." Then Jesus answered her, "O woman, great is your faith! Be it done for you as you desire." And her daughter was healed instantly. [Matthew 15:21-28]

A cartoon in a magazine showed a woman preacher speaking from the pulpit. Two middle-aged portly men were seated near the front. Looking up at the preacher, one of them said, "Nag, nag, nag." It is a truism that men do not like nagging women. In his *Journal* John Wesley tells of some Methodists who were arrested for disturbing the peace with their prayers. They were brought to court and the judge asked what the charges against them were. One reported, "Your honor, they pretended to be better than other people; and besides, they prayed from morning to night. And what's more, they even converted my wife. Until she started going among Methodists, she had such a tongue! And now she is quiet as a lamb." The judge shouted, "Let them go! Let them all go and convert all the nagging wives in town!"

In today's Gospel lesson Jesus and the disciples were confronted with a nagging woman. They came to Jesus with the demand, "Get that woman off our backs!" In the words of the text, they said, "Send her away, for she is crying after us." Is nagging a good thing? Should men take it up to get what they want? Nagging got results for the Canaanite woman. Her method persuaded Jesus to give what she wanted: the healing of her daughter severely possessed of demons. This is a problem for each of us. How do you get Jesus to help you and your loved ones? What can you do to get your prayers answered? Nag, nag, nag?

No Right To Nag

So, we must ask, should we nag God to get help or to have our prayers answered? In the first place, we must admit that we have no right at all to nag God. We are in the same position and condition as the Canaanite woman. She had no right to nag Jesus because she was a woman. She was of the wrong sex. Being a woman today may not be a handicap, because to a large extent women are now considered equals with men. Today's woman has come a long way. There is Ann Landers who has the largest reading audience in the world; in this no man can match her. The country knows about Barbara Walters as the first woman to get a million dollars a year as a TV news commentator. Chris Evert excels as a tennis player. Today we find women serving as judges, governors, ambassadors, Cabinet members with Carter, and ministers, with almost twenty percent of the students in seminaries being women. In fact, in some cases men are beginning to act too much like women. A man went to a sale in a men's department and the sale table was crowded with women. As he tried to get close to the table, he politely said, "Excuse me," "Pardon me," and "May I get through, please?" None of these worked. He stepped back and surveyed the situation. He noticed that the women flapped their arms like chickens. He decided to try the same technique. He went back to the table and started to elbow his way to the sale table. When he bumped one woman, she looked at him and asked, "Hey, why don't you act like a gentleman?" He replied, "I tried that but it didn't work. Now I am acting like a woman!"

In Jesus' day a woman had practically no standing. She was considered the property of her husband. She had not rights or privileges except these which her husband deemed to grant her as a favor. She was a non-person. This attitude prevails today in some countries. A recent visitor to India tells how a Muslim woman can be divorced by her husband for not bearing children. All he needs do is to say three times, "I divorce you." Then she must go her way and earn her own living by begging on the streets. Because she was a woman, the lady in our text had no right to ask Jesus for any help whatsoever. Nevertheless, Jesus treats her as a person. His love and concern go beyond sexuality. In his mind, there is something more important than a person's sex. Paul put it this way: "In Christ there is neither male or female . . ."

The woman had no right to nag Jesus, because she was not only a woman but she was a Canaanite. The Canaanites were the original settlers when the Israelites came to claim the Promised Land under Joshua. For centuries the Canaanites were the hated enemies of the Jews. Because she was of the wrong race, she had no right to nag Jesus, nor to ask him for any favor. She had no claim on him as though he were her fellow-countryman. She was, in her day, a racial and national outcast undeserving of a Jew's help.

Isn't it strange that today we often have the same attitude toward those of another race and nation? We tell Polish jokes with glee at the expense of the Poles. With scorn we express our anti-semitism by calling them "kikes." Sad, to say, there are still white churches who refuse to accept black people as members. When Jimmy Carter was elected president, his Baptist church in Plains, Georgia, had a closed-door policy to blacks. After much controversy, the church eventually agreed to consider blacks for membership. Because the pastor was in favor of accepting members of all races, he was pressured to resign. Even though a church may officially have an open-door policy in accepting people as members regardless of race, there are many churches who treat non-whites with such coldness and unfriendliness that a member of a different race would not want to belong to that church. If that is the case, what good is it to have it on the books that the church is a house of prayer for all peoples?

Jesus' treatment of the Canaanite woman helps us to see what Jesus' attitude is toward those of a different race and nation. Jesus is open to and is willing to help anyone regardless of race, nation, or color of skin. Christianity is not an external but an internal relationship; it deals with the heart and not the body. If a person's heart is clean and right, it does not matter what the body is like. It is hard for many of us to get it into our heads that God loves all people, that Christ died for all people, and that it is God's will to have all men of every class and race, of every nation on earth, come to him for eternal life and peace. It may be shocking that God is not the God of white people only. Does it surprise you that God loves communists as well as capitalists? Are you a modern Jonah who became angry when God forgave the Ninevites, bitter enemies of the Jews?

The woman in our Gospel for today had no right to nag Jesus for the healing of her daughter. She had no right because she was a woman and a Canaanite. Moreover, she was a Gentile. She had the wrong religion. The disciples could say to Jesus, "Send her away, because she is not one of us." Jesus tried to get this message across to the woman when he said, "I was sent only to the lost sheep of the house of Israel." This woman was a pagan, a Gentile. In Jesus' day, a Gentile was a lower than the lowest creature. A good Jew would not enter a Gentile's house, nor have a meal with one of them. There was no social fellowship, and conversation was kept to a minimum, just enough to transact business. Now this infidel, who is outside the household of faith, has the nerve to beg Jesus for help, for even a miracle of healing.

In Jesus' day the Jewish religion was for Jews only. They were, they claimed, the chosen people of God. They were the people of God by virtue of the covenant which made God their God and nobody else's. It was a shocking thing for Jews to see Jesus consorting with the "false" religion of the Gentiles. He fraternized with them, talked with them, and performed miracles to help them as in this case of the Canaanite woman. It was a revolutionary thing when Paul received the revelation that God included the Gentiles in his plan of salvation. Paul became the missionary to the Gentiles. Christ was understood to be for both Jews and Gentiles. When the Jews refused to accept Christ, the apostles gave the gospel to the Gentiles. In today's Second Lesson, Paul expresses the hope that the Gentiles' acceptance of the gospel would encourage the Jews also to accept Christ as Lord. When Jesus left the earth, he gave as his last command that the disciples should make disciples of all nations and baptize them in the name of the triune God.

What does this mean then to us today? Are we to let all religions go their own way without disturbing them with the Christian faith? Shall we ignore other religions? Shall we accept other religions as being equal to our own? As Jesus helped a woman of another religion, we who are modern disciples need to help people of other religions by acquainting them with the gospel of Jesus. At the heart of Christianity is a missionary zeal. No real Christian can truly say that he does not believe in missions. We have a story to tell and good news to share, news that no other religion has. It can mean redemption and release.

Good Reason to Nag

Though we, like the Canaanite woman, do not have a right to nag God for help, we do have a reason for nagging God. Our reason for nagging God is our love for people who need help and healing. You will note that the Canaanite woman was unselfish. She did not want anything for herself. If it were for herself, she would, perhaps, be out of order in nagging Jesus. She was begging in behalf of her daughter. Our text explains, "My daughter is severely possessed by a demon." Can there be anything worse than that? This mother was concerned about her child. She was compassionate. Love compelled her to nag Jesus for aid.

This love and concern for one's child is quite a contrast to what is happening today. One sub-freezing morning at 3:30 a.m. in Atlanta during the bitter Winter of 1977, a baby was found wrapped in an Indian blanket on the bottom of an apartment complex garbage dumpster. The newborn child was taken to a hospital where nurses named him "Baby Snow." In the same year a thirty-one-year old woman discovered a new-born baby in a shopping bag lying against a hedge in Brooklyn. Are these rare instances? According to three leading sociologists the American home is the most violent place in the country. They claim that one million kids are growing up with parents who use guns and knives on them.

If we have the compassion of the Canaanite woman, we would have reason to nag Jesus for help. Out of compassion we would use intercessory prayer to get God's blessing upon all unfortunate people. Babies need to be wanted, but many are not. In a poll taken by Ann Landers, seventy percent of the parents replied "No" to the question, "If you had to do it over again, would you have children?" Contrast this with the birth announcement that came to our house recently. It was in the form of a doughnut with the caption, "Another sweet thing." It was their sixth child! And they still wanted him!

Is there compassion in our hearts to make us cry out to Jesus in behalf of the sick, the aged, and the dying! Love will make us pray for them. We will visit them, and we will listen to them. One of today's greatest needs is to have someone who will take time to listen. The need for listening is so desperate that in Los Angeles there is a business firm which has trained people to serve patients in hospitals by listening to them at the rate of $7.50 per hour.

When it comes to the sinner, is there compassion in the church or just judgment? Do we look down upon those who made a mistake? Are we understanding and do we offer acceptance? How does the church treat the divorced person? How do church members feel about the unwed girl who has a baby? Do we shun those who are homosexuals? A woman in the dock district of a city had an illegitimate child. She later went to a women's meeting in the church. She liked it and went back, but the women did not like her. The minister came to her and told her not to come back. He explained that the other women knew about her and said that if she came, they would not come. With deep sorrow in her face, she asked, "Sir, I know I'm a sinner, but isn't there anywhere a sinner can go?" Well, what do you say: Is there a place where a sinner can go if not to church?

Humility is another reason for nagging God for help. We dare not be too proud to ask, to beg incessantly for divine mercy. The Canaanite woman could not be stopped begging by insults. To test her faith, Jesus referred to her as a "dog" and said it was not fair to throw the children's food to the dogs. This did not stop her from asking for help. She absorbed the insult and said she would, like a dog, be willing to take only crumbs. No one can be insulted when he is humble enough to consider himself nothing. You cannot say anything that is downgrading about a humble person, because he already feels he is that.

Our appeal to Christ is based upon our need of him, not on our praise. We are humble enought to admit we are in need and that we are not self-sufficient to take care of our problems and needs. Like the woman in the text we willingly get down on our knees in humility and simply plead, "Lord, help me." Who could say "No" to that?

Humility will not only lead you to asking for help but will encourage you to do simple, menial tasks. A customer once wrote to Stanley Marcus of the Neiman-Marcus store in Dallas, "There's a very nice-looking woman whom I frequently see in your store picking dead leaves from plants. Surely you can find a better position for a person of such obvious quality." In his reply he pointed out that the only higher position he could give the lady was his own position, because she was his mother, a member of the board of directors. It was not beneath Jesus to take a towel and basin and wash the feet of his disciples in the Upper Room. Is there anything "beneath" you because of your pride? It is the humble who ask, plead, and beg for God's favor.

Humility is the quality that will make you admit when you are wrong and will cause you to ask another's pardon. Carl Sandburg, in his book *Lincoln: The War Years*, tells about Colonel Scott who requested a leave to attend the funeral of his wife who accidently drowned. President Lincoln refused the request. Early the next morning Lincoln came to Scott's hotel room and admitted to the amazed officer, "I have had a regretful night and come now to beg your forgiveness." Then Lincoln took the officer in his own carriage to the steamship and sent him on his way to the funeral.

Also, it is faith that makes you persist in your nagging Jesus for help. It was the Canaanite woman's faith that at last brought success. Jesus marvelled at her faith and exclaimed, "O woman, great is your faith!" She firmly believed that Jesus could and would heal her daughter. She believed Jesus was the Messiah, "the Son

of David." She believed he had the power to make her
daughter well again. She believed he was a man of such
compassion that he would not refuse her. Her faith was
proved by her persistence. She would not stop asking.
She would not take "No" for an answer. In spite of
silence, in spite of insults, in spite of arguments, this
woman believed Jesus would help her.

It is persistence in prayer that brings results. The
Canaanite woman was doing the very thing Jesus taught
his disciples to do. He told them a story about a woman
who nagged a judge for justice and kept nagging until
finally the judge gave her what she wanted just to get
rid of her. Jesus said if a judge will do this, how much
more God will answer the prayers that keep coming to
him. He would not answer the request to get rid of you
but because he loved you, and wanted to help you. The
lesson is that we should never give up asking for divine
assistance. The one who gives up is the loser. A father
was trying to encourage his son by saying, "Don't give
up, don't ever give up!" The boy replied, "But, I can't
solve my problem." His Dad continued, "Remember, son,
the people who are remembered are those who didn't
give up — Robert Fulton didn't give up, Thomas Edison
never gave up, Eli Whitney never gave up, and look at
Isadore McPringle." "Who is Isadore McPringle?" asked
the boy. "See," said the father, "you never heard of him
— he gave up!"

To "nag, nag, nag" to get what you want is not
appreciated by most people. It is a way of getting you to
do something you do not want to do. And you resent it. It
is not that way with God. Christ taught and encouraged
us to nag God until we get what we need. Persistence in
asking is evidence of faith. And faith in Christ is what
brings results.

Jesus . . . Who?
Pentecost XIV

Now when Jesus came into the district of Caesarea Philippi, he asked his disciples, "Who do men say that the Son of Man is?" And they said, "Some say John the Baptist, others say Elijah, and others Jeremiah or one of the prophets." He said to them, "But who do you say that I am?" Simon Peter replied, "You are the Christ, the Son of the living God." [Matthew 16:13-16]
Supplementary text: Matthew 17:1-9

When Jimmy Carter first started campaigning for the presidency in 1976, the slogan in some parts of the country was "Jimmy — WHO?" He started out as one little known from a town which at the time did not even need a traffic light, Plains, Georgia. This is not the slogan today, for the world knows who Jimmy Carter is. Every day the press, radio, and TV tell the world what he says and does. He has climbed the mountain of political success and has reached the apex of power and prestige as the leader of the United States of America.

Do we know Jesus any better than Carter? Should our slogan be "Jesus — WHO?" That sounds like a foolish question, for you may be asking, "Who doesn't know Jesus?" Do we really know who Jesus is? "Who is Jesus?" was the question continually asked throughout his ministry. After his first sermon at Nazareth, the people were impressed and asked, "Who is he anyway? Is he not Joseph's son?" At Caesarea Philippi Jesus asked, "Who do men say that I am?" When Jesus came into Jerusalem on Palm Sunday and aroused the whole city by the parade with palm branches and hosannas, the people asked, "Who is this?" When Jesus was on trial before Pilate, the governor did not know who Jesus was, for he asked, "Are you the king of the Jews?"

Who can answer? Man cannot, because each gives a different answer. One says he is John the Baptizer, another — Elijah, another — Jeremiah, another — "that prophet," and another and another ad infinitum. In our first text Peter answers rightly, "You are the Christ, the Son of the living God." But Jesus points out that he did not say this of himself but God gave the answer to him. Peter did not understand his answer because immediately he discouraged Jesus from going to the cross and Jesus had to call him the mouthpiece of Satan. It was not until the Transfiguration, six days later, when the three chosen disciples realized who Jesus was. He was transfigured by the glory of God. His clothes became white and his face shone like the sun. Two holy figures, Moses and Elijah, appeared and talked with Jesus, and God's voice thundered from the heavens, "This is my beloved Son." Jesus — WHO? God says "Jesus, my beloved Son."

There you have the answers. Jimmy who? Jimmy Carter, president of the USA. Jesus — who? Jesus, Son of God and Son of Man. In the area of the state, we have a man on the mountaintop of power, prestige, and authority — the pinnacle of political success. In the area of the spirit, Jesus — the very top, associate of the greatest saints of the past, and Son of God! How do people feel when men reach heights of power and glory? What is your reaction to Carter's election and Jesus' transfiguration?

Surprise!

One reaction is surprise. The hometown folks in Plains who have known the Carters for generations were really surprised when he was elected. One said, "I didn't think he had it in him." He was one of them, a peanut farmer like many of them. He was seen in the country store and worshiped in a small Baptist church, as many of them did. What did Jimmy know about world conditions? How could he know enough to run this country? The people were surprised that anyone from such humble surroundings could be elevated to the top office of the land.

This element of surprise was experienced by the Disciples on Mt. Hermon where the Transfiguration took place. They lived with Jesus for almost three years. They ate and drank and slept with him like any other person. They heard him laugh and saw his tears. How could they help but be surprised when they saw him transformed into a heavenly being with clothes as white as light and whose face beamed like the sun? They were surprised that this could be happening to the peasant of Nazareth, the son of a carpenter.

They should not have been surprised because Jesus was always surprising them. One night when the Disciples were crossing the Sea of Galilee they saw a figure which they thought was a ghost. They were scared to death, but Jesus called to them and revealed his identity. He was walking on the water toward them. Were they surprised that a human being could walk on water!

At another time he surprised them. A crowd of people needed to be fed. He told the Disciples to feed them with five loaves and a couple of fish. Their response was, "How can we feed so many with so little?" He told the Disciples to distribute the bread and fish, and that bread and fish kept stretching and stretching until all five thousand were filled with twelve baskets left over. What a surprise that was!

The biggest surprise Jesus gave them was on Easter. Jesus was nailed to a cross. His body was placed in a cave. The door was shut and sealed. They were sure that this was the end, just as death and burial are the end for every human. Were they surprised on the third day when the tomb was empty and the resurrected Jesus came to their meeting! This is the surprise that changed the world.

Jesus is still surprising people. You can be surprised at the power Christ can give you to face your needs and problems. At a testimonial meeting a young woman rose and said, "Through this revival I found Jesus Christ and he made me able to forgive the man who murdered my father." You would be surprised what strength can come to your life to do impossible things when you let Jesus come into your life.

You can be surprised, too, with what Jesus can do with your life if you turn your life over to him. He can take the shabby, the left-over lives, the garbage and transform them into something beautiful. Last year we had several meetings on the campus of Union College in Barbourville, Kentucky. We met a young Baptist preacher who formerly played the piano in a Manhattan nightclub band. Now he was directing a youth summer camp in the hills. He took us out to see it. For six months no one was there. Everything was in disarray and dirty. In a corner was an upright piano that took a beating at the hands of the youth. The casing was only half on and the ivory was off many of the keys. The young preacher found an old chair, sat down at the piano, and began to play as you seldom hear a piano played. The whole place took on a glory and you felt you were in a sumptuous concert hall. Your life might be battered like the piano, but when the Master virtuoso plays it, it is transformed into something lovely.

The key to it all is that if you let Christ take over your life, you might be surprised what he can do with it. In a cathedral in Europe, an organist was practicing one day. A man approached the console and asked if he could play a little. He looked like a bum. His appearance was that of a tramp. The organist at first refused, but the "bum" kept asking for the opportunity. At last the organist let him try to play. At once the fingers danced on the keyboard and glorious music was heard. When he was finished, the organist asked who he was. The stranger replied simply, "Felix Mendellsohn." After the great artist departed, the organist said to himself, "Just think, I amost did not let the master play." The Master, Jesus, wants to take over the console of your life and bring forth melody that will surprise you.

Proud!

When a common, ordinary man reaches the heights, the people around him react in another way — pride. This was the way the people of Plains, Georgia, felt when Jimmy was elected to the presidency. They shared his success and glory. They were proud to have a Georgian for the first time to be president of the nation. He was their Jimmy, and they were as proud as parents. By the thousands they went to his inauguration — in trainloads, busloads, and in car caravans. They watched his induction with great pride. My Barbara shares that pride. While he was campaigning, she wrote him a letter telling him she was praying for him. He sent her a personal letter in return. And is she proud of this letter! If at anytime I suggest that maybe Jimmy might do better in this or that, she quickly comes to his defense saying, "Now remember, he is your president!"

The Disciples reacted with pride when they learned who Jesus was on Mt. Transfiguration. They were proud that God transformed him into the brightness of the sun. They were proud that Jesus was among the greatest of God's prophets. When God spoke from the clouds saying Jesus was his beloved Son, the buttons of their vests, if they had any, popped from pride in their man, their friend. This pride was expressed when Peter said, "If you wish, I will make three booths here, one for you, one for Moses, and one for Elijah." The Disciples wanted to keep them together and with them for always.

Maybe you are surprised that pride is suggested as a reaction, because you usually think of pride as being a cardinal sin. Well, it is if it is the wrong pride. When you are proud of yourself, it is a sin. A businessman was interviewed by a newspaper reporter. The reporter asked, "Did I understand you to say that you were born in a log cabin?" "No," said the businessman, "you have me confused with Abraham Lincoln. He was born in a log cabin; I was born in a manger." But, when you are proud of others, it is a good kind of pride. This was the pride the people of Plains and the Disciples had. .

We do have reason to be proud of Jesus. You and I can be proud of his courage shown when he was threatened by King Herod. Jesus refused to flee even though it was reported that Herod was out to kill him. He replied, "Tell that fox": I am going to stay here and do my work, and when my work is done I will move on! You have to be proud of courage like that.

We can be proud of Jesus for the way he handled the woman caught in adultery. Religious leaders were about to stone her to death. It was a delicate situation, but how beautifully Jesus handled it. He told them, "He who is without sin cast the first stone." At the same time he gave the woman assurance of forgiveness and told her to sin no more. He not only saved a life but he won a soul that day. We can be proud of one like that!

When Jesus' enemies came to trick him with their insoluable questions, he answered in such a way that we can be proud of him. They brought him the tricky matter of church and state by asking if taxes should be paid to Caesar. You remember the answer that has been repeated down the centuries, "Render to Caesar . . . render to God . . ." Then there was the impossible question, which of all the thousands of laws was the greatest. Without hesitation, he simply answered, "Love God with all your heart and your neighbor as yourself."

Are you as an individual proud of Jesus today? Could you be ashamed of him when you are with a secular crowd who does not go for church and Jesus? Do you keep silent and not let anyone know you are a Christian and active church member? Do you deny him among your social circle or among your business associates? One summer a young Christian went to work in the northwest with lumber jacks. When he came back he told how tough they were: obscene language, filthy stories, constant cursing and swearing. They laughed at God and thought Christ was a sissy. His friend asked, "How did you, a Christian, get along with them?" He replied, "Just fine. They never found out I was a Christian."

Are you ashamed to mention Jesus' name when you pray in public? Are you afraid you might offend Jews, secularists, atheists, and agnostics by praying in Jesus' name? I, for one, am so very proud of Bishop William R. Cannon who had the inaugural prayer for Jimmy Carter. At the end of his prayer, he said, "All this we ask in the name of Jesus Christ, thy Son and our Savior. Amen." This was on national TV and radio networks. Not only most of the nation but much of the world was hearing and seeing. I am proud of a Bishop who would let the whole world know where he stood in his relationship with Christ. Are you that brave, that Christ-centered, or are you ashamed to mention his name in public?

Awe!

When a person reaches the top in power and prestige, in authority and glory, people usually react in a third way, with awe. It is not the same in Plains since Jimmy came back home after the inauguration. Instead of a peanut farmer and close neighbor, he was now the mighty president of the United States. No longer would they address him as "Jimmy" but as "Mr. President." As he walked in the peanut fields, and sat in a pew in the little frame church on Sunday, those who saw him and were near to him felt a certain amount of awe, respect, and unworthiness. Recently there was carried in a Lutheran paper a picture of a group from Columbus, Georgia who came to Plains to visit the Carters. In the middle of the picture was Jimmy Carter seated and a little boy was standing between his legs and Jimmy's arms were around him. This boy happened to be the son of a Lutheran pastor in Columbus. Can you imagine how thrilled the boy and his father were? All the rest of his life, the boy will treasure that picture and relive the experience. For how many of us ever had a president's arms around us? That's even better than sitting on Santa's lap!

The Disciples had this reaction to learning that Jesus was the Son of God as revealed on Mt. Transfiguration. They were dazzled with the bright light of Jesus' presence. They were in the presence of holy men, Moses and Elijah. They heard the voice of God thundering from heaven, "This is my beloved Son." They fell on their faces and were struck with a sense of awe. Jesus came and touched them saying, "Rise and have no fear." This is a normal reaction to experiencing the divine. How would you react if you really heard the voice of God? Once there was a half-wit who had the habit of going to a barn every evening, taking off his hat, and saying, "Howdy God, I am here." Then he would begin to preach to an empty barn. Some pranksters plotted to pull a trick on him. They hid in the barn, and when he said, "Howdy God, I am here", with a deep voice they answered, "Howdy, Jim, I am here." Well, Jim dropped his hat and took off, and never again was he seen at the barn.

When we confront the holiness of Jesus as Peter did, we will have a sense of awe and unworthiness before the purity and perfection of Christ. Peter fell on his knees and said, "Depart from me, Lord, for I am a sinful man." Haven't we in the church lost something of this unworthiness in the presence of the holy Christ? It is not uncommon to hear no confession of sins in a worship service. If you come to the pure Jesus, why do you not instinctively say, "God, be merciful to me, a sinner"?

If we would come face to face with the greatness of Jesus, we would be filled with awe, too. This greatness can be seen in his power. When Jesus and the Disciples were on the Sea of Galilee, a storm came up but Jesus was asleep. The winds howled and the waves banged against the boat, and water was getting inside the boat. They thought they would drown. They awakened Jesus who stood up and addressed the winds and waves, "Peace, be still." Then the winds became calm and the sea was like a mountain lake. What was their reaction? They said to each other, "What manner of man is this that even the winds and the waves obey him?"

Experience the goodness of Christ and you will bow down before him in reverence. There was a woman who was cleansed and healed by Jesus. When he was having dinner in a friend's home, she came and sat at his feet. She washed his feet with her tears of gratitude and wiped his feet with her hair. This was a most humble act, for if you know what a woman's hair means to her, you know how demeaning it was to dry his feet with her hair. When you have experienced the mercy, love, and acceptance of Jesus, you are amazed at his grace. You bow down to worship him.

Isn't there something strange about the average church? It is supposed to be the House of God, a holy place, where God is present in spirit through the Word and Sacraments. Yet, we do not act or talk as though God is really here. What has happened to our respect for holy places? Where is our reverence for God's House? What has happened to the sense of awe and adoration in the worship service? Is God not here with us? Is Christ not present? Or are they here but we are too stupid to sense their presence? It is a universal experience that when men and women stand in the presence of the Holy, they are overcome with a feeling of awe.

Jimmy — Who? That is no longer the question, because the world knows Jimmy Carter is president of the United States. Jesus — who? Is that an unnecessary question, too? No, the world does not really know Jesus. That is proved by the world's lack of love and obedience to Jesus. To know Jesus is to love him and to die for him. How is the world to know who Jesus is? When Jesus led the Disciples down from the Transfiguration, he commanded they should tell no one who he was, as revealed on the mountain, until he was raised from the dead. Today we seem to be living before rather than after the cross. Now that Jesus died and rose again, we have a mandate to give a message to the world. It is: Want to know who Jesus is? He is the Christ, the Son of the living God. This is God's answer to "Jesus — WHO?" Is it also yours? Then tell the world with joy!